W9-BXN-122

THE UNITED STATES OF BEER

ALSO BY DANE HUCKELBRIDGE

Bourbon: A History of the American Spirit

THE

OF

A FREEWHEELING HISTORY OF THE ALL-AMERICAN DRINK

DANE HUCKELBRIDGE

WILLIAM MORROW
An Imprint of HarperCollinsPublishers

HarperCollins books may be purchased for educational, business, or sales promotional use. For information, please e-mail the Special Markets Department at SPsales@harpercollins.com.

FIRST EDITION

Designed by William Ruoto

Image on page vii courtesy AP Photo/Spina.
Images on pages 12 and 14 courtesy Boston Beer Company.
Images on pages 16, 25, 29, 47, 48, 60, 64, 71, 100, and 197 courtesy Wikimedia Commons.
Images on pages 91, 97, 115, 117, 140, 144, 168, 178, 180, 182, 183, 184, 194, 200, 203, 204, 212, 214, 220, 223, 225, 244, and 247 (top) courtesy Library of Congress.
Images on pages 233, 235, 256, and 257 courtesy Anchor Brewing Company.

Library of Congress Cataloging-in-Publication Data has been applied for.

ISBN 978-0-06-238975-6

16 17 18 19 20   OV/RRD   10 9 8 7 6 5 4 3 2 1

You can't be a real country unless you have a beer and an airline. It helps if you have some kind of a football team, or some nuclear weapons, but at the very least you need a beer.

— FRANK ZAPPA

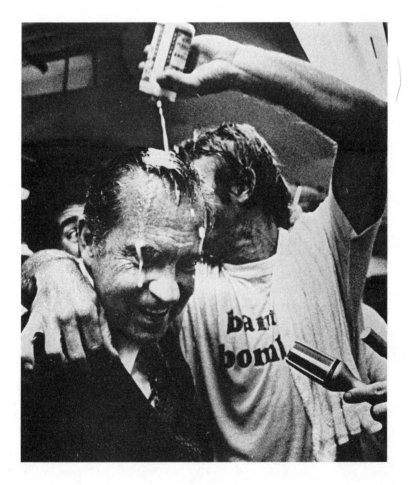

Contents

THE UNITED STATES OF BEER

E PLURIBUS, BREWDOG

"BEER," AS BENJAMIN FRANKLIN ALLEGEDLY QUIPPED, "is proof that God loves us and wants us to be happy." It may indeed be that—you won't encounter any debate on that point here—but it is a great many more things to our nation as well. To name just a few: Beer is the carbonated motor in a quarter-*trillion*-dollar American industry. Today it is second only to water and soft drinks when it comes to popularity among beverages, even beating out such staples as coffee and milk. It is a brew made for bonding, a point of local pride, and most important for our purposes, a beloved and reoccurring character in the story of a country. Disembark with the Pilgrims at Plymouth Rock, march with George Washington, or ride with Paul Revere, and what will you find? Why, you'll find beer. It is a relative constant in a multifarious culture, and a liquefied shibboleth for a people—or perhaps more accurate, conglomeration of peoples—who have been throughout the course of their history notoriously difficult to box in or pin down. Malt, yeast, and hops have formed a glue of sorts, perhaps not the only one, yet a surprisingly important binding ingredient. And in their many diverse expressions, they have enabled a variegated set of hyphenated identities to adhere, admirably if not perfectly.

Indeed, we Americans have never been shy about touting the richness of our own diversity—in theory, anyway. Native Americans and explorers alike recognized the great abundance of our wildlife and the shimmering beauty of our varying landscapes. Immigrants and early settlers brought to our shores a wealth of creeds and a bounty of tongues, all of which shaped the multifaceted character of our nation, as they continue to do. It's written smack-dab on our currency, for Pete's sake. *E Pluribus, Unum*: From Many, One. Even in they didn't always put it in practice, our founding fathers recognized the value of this inclusion, which preserved our Union when it teetered on the brink of collapse. No, a house divided against itself cannot stand. But an ideal of life, liberty, and the pursuit of happiness, propped up by a colorful caste of dreamers and doers from every far-flung corner of the globe—you needn't a powdered wig or a stovepipe hat to recognize that *that* makes for one hell of story. And possibly, a civilization quite unlike any other, in history or on earth.

Difference, as an abstract notion, is stitched into the fabric of the American experience—though there have always been a few rips and tears. The Mohegan Indians never did care much for the more entrepreneurial Pequots. English Puritans could barely stomach the free-wheeling Dutch. And the voluptuary habits of French-speaking Creoles made stuffier minds in Washington wonder if the Louisiana Purchase had even been worth it. Geechees and Gullahs spoke a coastal southern dialect unintelligible to their inland kin, Tejanos in the Southwest confused the heck out of the Anglos with their fandangos, and when it comes to the Amish sects of the Pennsylvania Dutch, they've been perplexing the rest of motor-loving America for the better part of a century.

And yet despite all our differences and affiliations, a common thirst for beer has prevailed, enjoyed consistently across the many years and layers of the American experience. That golden alchemy of barley and hops was as precious to the pilgrims and patriots of yore as it is to the Joe Six-Packs of today, with a dependable, practically culture-defining ubiquity. True, there is baseball and pop music, but both are relatively recent arrivals compared to the beloved brewdog, and neither tastes so good after mowing the lawn on a hot summer day.

Are we being cheeky or melodramatic, to attach so much drama and import to such an everyday drink? Perhaps. But it's worth looking at the numbers. Just how much do we love beer? About six billion gallons worth—that's the amount of beer Americans consume on a yearly basis, with each drinking-age adult chugging back an average of nearly thirty gallons of pilsner, lager, porter, and ale. That number is impressive, and it stays relatively consistent across the board, whether you're in Alabama or Alaska, California or the District of Columbia. And that's in the present day, mind you. Take a glance at the drinking habits of the early colonial period or the Industrial Revolution—which we shall be doing in short order—and one simple and undeniable fact emerges: America is a nation of beer drinkers. We always have been, to varying degrees, and we most likely always will be.

As for explanations of beer's ubiquity across the length and breadth of American civilization, there are several obvious avenues one might pursue. For starters, the role it has played in civilization itself. Wine may get the credit these days as the most "civilized" drink, but the brewing of beer and the cultivation of grains—the latter of which allowed our ancient forbearers to give up hunting and gathering and start watching college football in those newfangled things called cities—share a relationship that's practically symbiotic. It's impossible to say precisely when ancient humans first realized that a bowl full of bread left out in the rain might ferment into something intoxicatingly delicious, but pictorial and written evidence suggests that barley beer was widespread throughout the Near East by 4000 B.C., and very well may have existed in the Fertile Crescent as far back as 10,000 B.C. Sumerians lauded beer in the *Epic of Gilgamesh*, Mesopotamians were known to drink it through straws, Egyptian pharaohs consumed it on a daily basis, and Sophocles himself believed beer should be enjoyed frequently, albeit in moderation, and with plenty of bread and meat on the side. The Chinese discovered the recipe for malted rice-based beer almost ten thousand years ago, millet and sorghum-based brews have been well known to Africans since time immemorial, and multiple Native American civilizations—whose forebearers discovered America via the Bering Strait many thousands of years before Columbus stumbled upon the West Indies—have been incorporating corn beer into their feasts and rituals for thousands of years. Almost since the beginning, it seems, beer has rivaled water as the universal beverage.

Then there is also the basic fact of nutrition. Despite what junior high health class would lead you to believe, beer is actually brimming with precisely the sort of things a body needs to be healthy. In addition to its pure energy potential—between 100 and 300 calories per pint, depending on the style and consistency—most beers also contain considerable amounts of readily digested peptide-based proteins, soluble glucan-based fiber, minerals such as potassium, calcium, and magnesium, and a ton of essential water-soluble vitamins. Even the alcoholic portion of beer, although obviously deleterious when consumed in large quantities, has been suggested to improve heart health and increase lifespan when enjoyed in moderation. Our historical predecessors may not have been well educated on the chemical specifics of the beer they consumed, but they were well aware of the crucial role it played in their diets, especially during leaner historical periods when food was scarce and clean water difficult to come by. Beer, they found, filled in for both quite nicely.

So is that it then? Simply a matter of wholesomeness and heritage? Possibly so. But then again, milk is also brimming with vitamins and minerals, yet old friends seldom go out to grab a glass of 2 percent and catch up. Wine and whiskey have an equally illustrious history, but no U.S. president ever hosted a Pinot Noir Summit at the White House to help smooth out our differences; no baseball vendor ever enlivened a season opener with cries of "get your ice-cold bourbon, here." What makes beer feel so distinctly and consistently American?

It is a question that I must admit, I seldom considered before beginning this book. Granted, I had been drinking beer for the entirety of my adult life—even longer if you count a few childhood sips and adolescent shenanigans. In Ohio, I had grown up around the canned domestic macrobrews that form the backbone of the beer industry in America, and some of my earliest memories are of begging my father—usually with little success—for a tinny taste of his forbidden Bud. As a young writer gone east, I buttressed that midwestern foundation further with a selection of local craft brews and preferred imports (I've always had a weakness for Chimay, and when the weather's warmer, I seldom turn down a good hoppy IPA). To doubt the seminal role beer plays in our culture would have been tantamount to questioning the Rockies or Lake Erie or the Mighty Mississip—it had always been there, had it not? It was one of those things that an American just takes for granted.

That was until, on a whim, I decided to dabble in a little brewing of my own. Ironically, my initial interest in the home production of alcoholic beverages was not related directly to beer, but rather whiskey. Having just completed a history of bourbon in America, I thought it might prove educational to engage in a little moonshining of my own—only to discover that a host of legal impediments stood in the way when it came to spirits. For reasons of taxation and safety, home distillation was subject to regulations that had been on the books since Prohibition. Beer, on the other hand, was essentially fair game, as it had been since 1979, when its own Prohibition-era restrictions on home brewing were finally lifted. As long as it is for personal consumption and not sale, any adult can brew his or her own beer. Seeing as how whiskey is at its essence little more than distilled beer, and considering the fact that I was more than happy to drink either one, I rolled up my sleeves and gave brewing a try.

First, there were a few problems to solve: I had no recipe, no equipment, and none of the supplies. I knew little beyond the basics—that beer was the result of a specific yeast strain making alcohol and carbon dioxide out of the natural sugars of a malted grain. This, and the truth that, if done properly, it tasted pretty damn good. Fortunately, I had a brother-in-law in our nation's capital—here's to you, Steve—who dabbled in home brewing and had a passion for good beer. In fact, he once went so far as to use the Freedom of Information Act to request the secret recipe for White House Honey Ale. And while it did not yield the top secret information he desired, it does speak to the lengths he'll go to to find the finest suds around.

So, on one fine spring day, I caught the train from New York to Washington, D.C., browsing en route Charlie Papazian's seminal work *The Complete Joy of Homebrewing* to nail down the basics. Just as I'd hoped, the afternoon proved extremely educational. I learned about steeping the barley, boiling the wort, pitching the yeast, and sanitizing the carboy, all while sampling a heady assortment of American beers. *It takes beer to make beer,* as the old brewer's adage goes, and Steve had supplied us with a full range of craft brews to enjoy when the brewing began. There was Stoudts Pils from Pennsylvania, Left Hand Milk Stout from Colorado, Great Lakes Dortmunder Gold from Ohio, Abita Turbodog from Louisiana, Devils Backbone Vienna Lager from Virginia, Firestone Walker Wookey Jack from California, Dogfish Head Palo Santo Marron from Delaware—the eclectic list went on and on, with each seemingly more delicious than the last.

The conversation eventually turned philosophical, as those enriched by good beer so often do, and the aforementioned questions of beer's unique role in American history and culture came to be asked. And gradually, confronted by that diverse array of American brews before us, an undeniable fact emerged: this "national" drink of ours wasn't national at all. That truth may have been obscured by the rise of ubiquitous national brands in the twentieth century, but beginning with the earliest American settlers, and continuing on up to the craft brews of the present day, beer has been and still is a local phenomenon. It may be enjoyed across the nation, but for most of our history, it's been made next door. Our affection for beer is common and universal, but its history in our country is exceptionally regional. And thanks to its regional origins, as I would come to discover in the days that followed, the experiences of early brewers would help shape the unique history and identity of our country in a myriad of surprising ways.

How so? Well, for beginners, in New England, the Puritans' beer not only brought the *Mayflower* to shore and the minutemen to arms, it also helped establish Harvard and Yale, and, one could argue, paved the way for college football. In Manhattan, a tradition of entrepreneurial, trade-oriented brewing that first arrived with the Dutch would eventually give rise to Babe Ruth and the New York Yankees. In the Midwest, beer garden contests between rival German American factions would give birth to amusement parks and roller coasters, and in the South, the same improvised beer recipes Jamestown settlers experimented with when their barley wilted would set the stage for American whiskey. It was a novel idea, and an intriguing one at that—the notion that local beers actually helped to shape the distinctive regional cultures that would cohere and combine to build a nation. Beer, like America, has prevailed not because of uniformity, but rather diversity—and it has always allowed for interpretation at the local and regional level to accommodate it. Essentially, everyone loves beer . . . but opinions have always varied as to what beer should be.

Needless to say, for someone with an interest in American history and a love of good drink, it seemed an issue that warranted further exploration. "How long until this home brew is ready to drink?" I asked my brother-in-law Steve, basking in the sun and sipping on my second Great Lakes Dortmunder Gold of the day. "About a month" was his nonchalant reply.

And at that moment, flush with that distinctly American brand of naive optimism, not to mention a half-dozen exceptionally good beers consumed over the course of a beautiful spring day in our nation's capital, that short interval felt like just enough time.

Little did I know.

CHAPTER 1

NEW ENGLAND

or

A Proper Happy Hour

for the *Mayflower*

AS A CHILD, ONE OF MY GREAT FANTASIES WAS GETTING to tour Willy Wonka's chocolate factory. It was crushing to learn that, no, there are no golden tickets hiding in Wonka bars, and no eccentric geniuses willing to let you sample their most experimental creations. But as an adult, I have discovered that a private tour of the original Sam Adams research and development brewery in Boston, Massachusetts, comes pretty darn close to that dream. Chewing on chocolate-roasted malts, getting my hands sticky with lupulin, even catching a forbidden whiff of the mythic, wild yeast ale known as the Kosmic Mother Funk: sweet stuff for any lover of beer, or history, for that matter, because the brewery, built way back in 1870, practically leaks the stuff. The highlight of the tour comes at its conclusion, seated at the bar in the tasting room. It is a Friday, the brewers have just punched out for the day, and their stories begin to flow like the beer. The sort of inside scoop you don't usually get on the back of a bottle. Over a pint of original Boston Lager—the freshest, without a doubt, I've ever had—I learn that Rudolph Haffenreffer, who owned the facility long before it ever brewed Sam Adams, piped out the excess heat from the brew kettles to heat his own house. In the old days, I found out, there was a tap outside the building that was open to locals, and that Babe Ruth used to drop by for a quick mug or five. And that strange, truncated smokestack with only half of the brewery's original name along its side? Hurricane Gloria lopped the top clean off in 1985, and it's read FENREFFER BREWERS ever since.

The Boston Beer Company's R&D brewery is located at the original headquarters of Haffenreffer beer, in the Jamaica Plain neighborhood of Boston, Massachusetts. Legend has it that Babe Ruth and his Red Sox teammates used to swing by for pails of Haffenreffer.

There is one story, however, recounted over these end-of-the-day pints, that I find even more incredible than the rest. I hear it from brewer Dean Gianocostas, who has been at Sam Adams since the mid-'80s, back when it, alongside a few upstarts on the West Coast, was the only American craft alternative to the brewing behemoths. Still, it's hard for me to believe. How could the Boston Lager I'm currently drinking, the beer that effectively started a revolution and altered the landscape of American brew culture forever, have had its origins not in some Old World beer academy or state-of-the-art testing room, but rather in an attic, buried beneath a stack of old *Motor Trend* magazines? Yes, *Motor Trend*. Apparently, this was where Jim Koch, the creator of Samuel Adams beer and founder of the Boston Beer Company, discovered his great-great-grandfather's recipe for a distinctive style of lager. A beer of the sort Americans had once savored, in the days before Prohibition, but that had long since been forgotten. It truly was a different, older style of brew—one which eschewed "adjuncts" (fillers like corn, rice, or wheat) in favor of a higher-quality two-row barley, and called for rare varieties of noble hops to lend it some character. A beer that, lager yeast aside, was much more like the darker, hoppier, higher-gravity ales of New England's first settlers than the diluted pilsners that eventually came to supplant them. As something of a visionary—*and* a rebel—Jim Koch recognized this right away. And, if the story is to be believed, he also lost all his kitchen wallpaper in the process. According to Dean, the steam from brewing his first batch took it right off the walls.

I thank the brewers once the beers are done, and I make my way back downtown. I still have a couple hours to kill before my bus departs for New York, time enough for one more stop before leaving Boston: the Bell in Hand Tavern. Admittedly, it is something of a tourist stop, and yes, the flat-screen TVs don't lend themselves to historical reflection. But the place was built in 1795—just a dozen years after the American Revolution—and it doesn't take much imagination to envision what the bar must once have been. It was in taverns just like this that the first rumblings of independence began, as men like Sam Adams and John Hancock capitalized on an age-old English tradition of airing gripes and planning next steps in the local alehouse. The bartender asks me what I'd like, and I see that Sam Adams brews a special colonial-style ale just for the Bell in Hand. I order one, with a bowl of chowder to go with it, and with the first taste of the pint, realize that perhaps the story Dean told me about the origins of Boston Lager isn't so far-fetched after all. If American democracy itself could have been born over mugs of beer in a humble tavern such as this, maybe a long-lost family recipe could have ignited the flame that would reintroduce regional craft beer to the American mass market.

A young Jim Koch in front of an early batch of his signature Samuel Adams Boston Lager. In the 1980s, he helped reintroduce our nation to a revolutionary idea: that American beer could actually have character.

But with such a good tale, I have to know for sure. And as soon as I get back to New York, I can't help but ask Jim Koch himself. Did Sam Adams really begin up in an attic, buried beneath a stack of old magazines?

"This is all true!" comes his enthusiastic reply. "In 1984, I told my father I was going to quit my job as a consultant to become a brewer. He looked at me and said, 'Jim, you've done some stupid things in your life. That's just about the stupidest.'" This, according to Jim, wasn't an unexpected reaction—the Koch family had been making beer for generations, and his father, who worked as a brewmaster for a regional beer maker, had seen small breweries fold by the dozens. Making carefully crafted, old-fashioned beer in a market dominated by mass-produced macrobrews seemed doomed to fail. Nevertheless, the elder Koch took his headstrong son up to the attic where the family kept its old records, and, more important, where a few of the family beer recipes could still be found. This included, as it turned out, his great-great-grandfather's Louis Koch Lager—the beer that would eventually become the Boston Lager we know today. And the wallpaper? Jim has an answer for that as well. "When I brewed my first batch in my kitchen, two things happened," he tells me. "The steam peeled the wallpaper off the walls, and I fell in love with the taste of this beer which came to be known as Samuel Adams Boston Lager."

Yes, revolutions can begin in rather unexpected places—and when Jim Koch pulled that brittle piece of paper out from beneath stacks of *Motor Trend* (and, I learn, *Road & Track*) to create Sam Adams, he didn't just resurrect an old Koch family recipe—he reintroduced America to a significant piece of its own lost brewing heritage. With the return of darker malts, more aromatic hops, and eventually even ale yeast, he brought back to New England a tradition of beer making that had not begun in 1776, but much earlier, in a misty isle across the sea. To understand the history of beer in *New* England, we've got to make a quick stop in the *old* one.

The British Isles are the site of some of the oldest beer-related artifacts discovered in Europe—indeed, even the

Beer can be made from any number of grains, although in Britain and much of Europe, barley has always been the cereal of choice.

world. On pottery shards uncovered to the north in the Scottish Isle of Arran dated to 3000 B.C., scientists have detected traces of cereal and honey residue that point to beer consumption. Grooved pot fragments from Balfarg farther east, dating to the third millennium B.C., also indicate grain residue, as well as the pollen of henbane* and meadowsweet—ingredients known to be used as flavoring agents in alcoholic drinks in ancient times. And taking a cue from their Neolithic predecessors, Bronze and Iron Age Celtic Britons took to brewing with equal alacrity, a fact attested to by the generally alarmed observations of ancient scholars. In the fourth century B.C., the Greek explorer Pytheas wrote that these "barbarians" who lived in the more frigid parts of Britain prepared a concoction from honey and grain; several centuries later, another Grecian by the name of Dioscorides would describe how much British Celts relished chugging back a barley beer known as *kourmi*. T-shaped structures dated to the first century A.D. were almost certainly used as grain kilns and would have provided beer for the many feasts held in honor of great warriors. In short, the Brits have been beer enthusiasts since the very beginning.

Celtic Britons weren't the only Europeans who developed a strong hankering for British beer, though. One generally thinks of Romans as wine drinkers, but when Britain was added to their empire in the first century A.D., it didn't take Roman troops long to pick up on Celtic customs. The provincial soldiers who served in the Roman army were especially fond of local brews and often demanded them as part of their daily ration. Among the remains of the northern outpost of Vindolanda, a tablet was recovered from around A.D. 100 in which the decurion Masculus writes to the prefect Flavius Cerialis with the urgency of a Cancun spring breaker: "My fellow-soldiers do not have any *cervesa;* I request that you order some to be sent." Carbonized malted grain residue

---

*Interestingly, some scientists have noted the henbane plant, which is dangerous when consumed in larger doses, actually produces psychedelic effects when ingested in smaller amounts. Evidence, perhaps, that Neolithic Britons weren't just getting drunk—they were tripping.

at Roman fortress excavations in Bearsden and Caerleon indicate that not only did Caesar's legions stationed abroad drink large quantities of beer, they got so desperate for it they made it themselves—proof, if nothing else, that standing around guarding Hadrian's Wall all day was just as dull as it sounds.

The real history of English beer drinking, however, doesn't start until after the Roman Empire's collapse in the fifth century, with the appearance of a couple feisty Germanic tribes called the Angles and the Saxons. When Rome finally abandoned its British outposts, the indigenous Celts were left unprepared to deal with the warlike tribes of Picts and Gaels that leered at them menacingly from the island's wild fringes. Out of desperation, the British Celts invited Angles and Saxons as mercenaries to come across the Channel and help them out. And the arrangement of money-for-protection went off more or less without a hitch—until it became clear that, just like the Hells Angels at Altamont, these unruly Germanic bodyguards did not much appreciate being told what to do. One can almost imagine the tremendous lump in the Celtic king Vortigern's throat when he realized his belligerent, beer-guzzling guests were not only refusing to do as he asked, they were in fact bringing a few thousand of their kinsmen from northern Germany and southern Denmark to join them.* Battles between the native Celts and Anglo-Saxons would rage for centuries, with Celtic civilizations living on in Wales to the west and Scotland to the north. But "Angle-Land," as it came to be known, was born—a rather bellicose beginning for Jolly Old England.

---

*It is a compelling historical side note that beer very well may have played a starring role in the Anglo-Saxon conquest. While dining with Vortigern, the Anglo-Saxon leader Hengist plied the king with large quantities of wine and "other fermented drinks" to convince him that the district of Kent ought to be his, initiating their control of formerly Celtic lands. This author would wager that the drinks in question included copious quantities of beer.

But just who were these rowdy Anglo-Saxons? One might describe them as precursors to the Vikings. They hailed from the same northern Germanic world, they worshipped roughly the same pantheon of war-hungry gods, they plundered the same foreign lands, and most important for our purposes, they had the same robust thirst. The Anglo-Saxons drank a variety of beverages, including *wîn* (wine), *medo* (meade), *ealu* (ale), and *beor* (you can figure that one out on your own). Mead and wine were certainly feasting hall favorites, but they were upper-class drinks, perhaps even special-occasion tipples not unlike modern-day champagne; the honey needed to make mead was a rare commodity, and wine had to be imported at great cost from the warmer, more grape-friendly parts of the European continent.

But beer? That was the everyday, every man's drink. Anglo-Saxon lexicon wasn't overly concerned with alcoholic distinctions, and the terms *ealu* and *beor* were used interchangeably to mean various drinks made from fermented grains. What didn't vary was their love for the stuff. In the late ninth century A.D., Alfred the Great described "weapons and meat and ale and clothes" as the only thing an Englishman really needed. In the famously inscrutable Old English poem *Beowulf,* King Hrothgar—technically a Scandinavian, but described through an Anglo-Saxon lens—evokes Grendel's scorn by constructing his massive *beor* hall Heorot, where warriors boasted of their deeds over brimming *beor* cups. Inevitably, such bragging often ended in a good old-fashioned *beor* brawl, a central part of Anglo-Saxon life, and a source of concern for those in charge. King Ine of Wessex passed an eighth-century law that stated: "If, however, they quarrel at their drinking of *beor,* and one of them bears it with patience, the other is to pay 30 shillings as a fine." Oftentimes, though, the dispute went beyond what a few shillings could fix. The venerable chronicler Cynewulf would also condemn those bewitched by alcohol, writing that "drunk on *beor,* they renewed old grievances . . . being stricken with wounds, they released their souls to flit doomed away from their body." In Anglo-Saxon England, beer was a part of everyday social life, albeit one that could turn dangerous at the drop of a helmet.

In the centuries that followed, England changed immensely. The arrival of Christianity banished the old gods, the Norman conquest upset the social order, and the florishing of the High Middle Ages pulled the English further from the primordial murk of Grendel's moors. At last, it seemed, those rowdy Anglo-Saxon tribesmen had put on their tights, picked up their lutes, and come into the fold of pan-European culture. One thing that would not change was the English fondness for beer. Or *beers,* more accurately, because by the early Middle Ages, English brewing had evolved enough to provide them with a panoply of options. There was sweet ale, new ale, Welsh ale, double-brewed ale, clear ale, sour ale, honey ale, good ale . . . why, there was even a mild ale, which one can only imagine was akin to modern near beer. But they were all ales. By medieval times, that name had won out, used to describe the generally sweet, dark, alcoholic drink that the English preferred above all others. It wasn't especially hard to make, at least not on a smaller scale, in its most rudimentary form. Simple domestic ale brewing involved little more than steeping malted barley in boiling water to produce a sugary liquid called "wort," then pitching in a little yeast once the wort had cooled. A few days or weeks of fermentation, and Bob's your uncle: English ale. Cider was enjoyed to some extent in the southwest of England, and wine continued to be imported as the ritzy potation of the landed class. Ale, though, was akin to bread—something no Englishman could do without.

In medieval England, brewing was largely the domain of skilled women known as "brewsters" or "alewives." Everything changed, however, with the rise of cities and the arrival of hops. Mother Louse, pictured here, was one of the last of her kind.

Interestingly, it was not English*men* who were brewing it. While today the post of "brewer" may conjure images of bearded and beflanneled gentlemen, for most of the English Middle Ages, brewing was an occupation dominated by women. Due largely to rural divisions of labor at the time— women were unquestionably the bosses when it came to most grain-based preparations—brewing fell under the auspices of the lady of the house. Known as "brewsters" or "alewives," they produced ale primarily for their own households, but they would also sell their surplus to friends and neighbors. The practice was common and widespread. In a fourteenth-century account from Brigstock, Northamptonshire, three hundred women—roughly one-third of the women who lived on the estate—brewed and sold ale. A similar share of women brewed and sold ale in Wakefield, Yorkshire, and Alrewas, Staffordshire. Brewing was still a cottage industry, but there were hints of the demand that would eventually pave the way for alehouses and taverns—direct ancestors of the modern English pub. The burgeoning popularity of both formal drinking establishments and ale is demonstrated rather heroically by this quick census of London taverns from 1309: with a population of around eighty thousand inhabitants, the upstart capital had only 354 taverns specializing in imported wine; at the same time, the fast-growing city boasted some 1,330 brewshops offering good old-fashioned English ale. That's one ale seller for every sixty inhabitants.

As to how much volume the English consumed, it's difficult to say with any precision, but evidence indicates they drank the stuff like water—for good reason. England underwent profound changes in the wake of the Black Death that ravaged the country in the middle part of the fourteenth century. With a third of the population lost to the plague, labor shortages and redistribution of wealth helped give birth to a new urban class. Essentially, a nation of rural peasants suddenly became upwardly mobile. And as this new cohort of more skilled and savvy laborers coalesced, English cities formed alongside them. The upside was the end of Old English feudalism, and the birth of a more modern world that was beginning to bear at least some resemblance to our own. The downside? Filth. Townsfolk would pour out their sewage into any open body of water, while tanneries and other caustic businesses dumped their runoff wherever they could. English water quickly became unsafe to drink, and in its place, the English drank beer. The boiling associated with brewing went a long way in killing bacteria, even in the case of ales that had very little alcohol at all, making it a safe and nutrient-rich replacement for local water—something only the most poor and desperate Englishman would dare to drink.

Some estimates put the per capita daily consumption for medieval England at around a gallon, which may seem implausible, although there is evidence to back it up. A hospital for lepers in northern England doled out to its patients four liters of ale a day in the fourteenth century, and not too far away in Great Yarmouth, sailors were given a ration of 4.5 liters for each day they spent in service of the navy—that's more than a gallon to help brave the high seas. Those may be extreme examples, but ale was certainly consumed in large quantities, by men, women, and children alike. But does that mean entire households were perpetually inebriated? Did families that drank together *stay* together? Not exactly. Because while, yes, some certainly did overindulge in strong ale, most of what people consumed at the dinner table was very low in alcohol. A common English small ale may have only been 1 or 2 percent alcohol by volume, making it more than suitable as an everyday drink.

As one can imagine, this social upheaval had a profound effect upon brewing as well. Ale making, formerly the domain of rural women whose primary objective was domestic pro-duction, increasingly became commercialized and profession-alized. Sadly, this meant the majority of women were pushed out of the business, as male-dominated trade guilds took over. This change was especially pronounced in the urbanized southeast, or East Anglia, which abutted London and included many of its surrounding towns. Initially, female brewers did play a crucial and active role in the establishment of urban brewing as a respected trade; in a tally conducted in 1420 by the London Brewer's Guild of ale hucksters, more women are mentioned than men. Over the decade that followed, overall guild membership would consistently come out to roughly one woman for every three men and was very likely higher because many women brewers used their husbands' names as false fronts to gain easier admittance. But by the end of the fifteenth century, women would make up only 7 percent of the guilds, and most of those were widows of deceased male members. By the early 1500s, brewing guilds were composed almost entirely of men, as women were squeezed out of their traditional roles and unfairly relegated to more subservient and unskilled positions in alehouses and taverns—an unjust end, unfortunately, to the venerable history of the English brewster.

New, more technologically advanced methods of production also came into play in the new world of industrialized ale making. At its essence, brewing was still a matter of adding yeast to boiled malt and allowing it to ferment into an alcoholic drink. But to produce ale on a rapidly growing commercial scale, new materials and machinery were needed. Whereas a rural alewife would have made do with little more than a brew kettle and a stir stick kept in the kitchen, commercial breweries required separate brewing spaces to house their vast array of equipment. The will of a deceased fourteenth-century brewer gives some indication of what that might have included: "a brewhouse, three shops, two leaden vessels, a lead cistern, a tap-trough, a mashvat, a vat for letting unwanted matter settle out, a vat to hold the finished ale, tubs, and other utensils." An inventory from 1486 also includes twenty small tubs of yeast as well as a loose wooden frame with small openings or false bottom for the mash tun. And with so much

As the old feudal structure of England fell apart in the Black Death's wake, brewing transitioned from a domestic rural activity to a professional urban craft. Taverns and beer vendors became hallmarks of town life.

beer being made, some form of industry regulation became necessary for maintaining quality control. The new class of urban breweries may have been privately owned, but government oversight wasn't far behind, to ensure brewers weren't cutting corners to make a few extra pounds. To keep up with the rise in production, the position of royal "aletaster" or "aleconner" was added to the civil service roster, under the auspices of the very official-sounding Assize of Bread and Ale. In what may very well have been the greatest job in the history of the world, the aletaster's sole responsibility was to sample each batch of fresh brew and report back to the king if it was too watery, weak, or otherwise unsavory. And it appears such vigilance was necessary: for instance, in 1449, in the town of Oxford, nine brewers were found guilty of making weak beer and forced under oath to promise never to do it again.

The greatest change to English brew culture, however, was born not of plagues or cities or mechanical innovations but came courtesy of a small, mildly bitter relative of the cannabis plant. It's known to science as the comical-sounding *Humulus lupulus,* but it's far more familiar to us beer lovers as . . . (drumroll, please) . . . hops. And with its arrival, English ale was already well on its way to becoming New England beer.

The practice of adding flavoring agents to grain-based fermented drinks goes back thousands of years in Britain. We already know traces of henbane, honey, and meadowsweet were found on Neolithic drinking vessel fragments from various sites around the British Isles. Surviving documents from the medieval period show that ales were also brewed using additives such as bog myrtle, wormwood, heather, spruce sap, carline thistle, and tree bark, along with a host of other agents used for either flavoring or medicinal purposes. A substance called *gruit,* whose exact recipe has been lost to the ages, was at one point the dominant beer spice, used all across northern Europe to put some kick in the brews.

Initially the English were loath to add hops—a plant whose small, cone-shaped flowers were beginning to gain popularity across the Channel in the monasteries of Carolingian France. One of the earliest references to a hop-based beer comes courtesy of a statute from Adalhard the Elder, at the monasteries of St. Stephen and St. Peter in Corbie, France, from A.D. 822. In it, he insists that the porter ought to receive a portion of all hops given to the monastery as tithes, and in the event the porter's hop supply was still low, he might "acquire for himself as much as necessary from which to make his own beer." Hops also caught on in Germany, as suggested by an A.D. 860 mention of a "humilarium" (the fancy Latin term for hop garden) in the abbey of Freisingen. And why was this process of "hopping" beer adopted so quickly on the European continent? The twelfth-century writings of the abbess Hildegard of Bingen spell it out quite plainly: "In its bitterness it prevents spoilage in those drinks to which it is added, so that they can last much longer." Meaning, those food preservatives listed on the back of your soft drink are not just a recent phenomenon. Monks and abbesses figured out early on that the hop plant had some rather handy antimicrobial and preservative properties. Granted, without the benefits of modern chemistry and microbiology, they didn't understand the exact mechanism by which the hops preserved their beer, but through trial and error, they figured it out. As anyone familiar with Mendel and his bean plants can attest, the two things monks have historically had in copious amounts are free time and garden plots, which led to a great deal of experimentation. And thankfully for the beer fans of the world, those medieval monastics figured out that beer made with hops lasted longer and tasted pretty good, too.

Tasted good to them, mind you. Because just a quick boat trip away, the English would not suffer such a sacrilege as putting hops in their ale. Some have cited evidence from Old English poetry suggesting a natural English aversion to bitter drinks, but another explanation seems more likely. For while much of the medieval beer in northern France and Germany was being churned out by monasteries—large, efficiency-minded complexes that produced sizable quantities for an entire region—English ale remained, for most of the medieval period, a smaller domestic product brewed by alewives to be consumed in the home, with any surplus sold off to the neighbor or tavern next door.* And as such, the English were not overly concerned with batch consistency or spoilage. The bitterness of hops was then, as it is today, something of an acquired taste, and with their established traditions of localized rural brewing, the population of medieval England had no reason to acquire it. In fact, they loathed the stuff—at least, initially.

The prejudice against hops would last for quite some time. The first case of Continental-style hopped beer being made in England comes from the London City Letterbooks of 1391. Yet that didn't prevent hopped beer from being actually outlawed in Norwich in 1471, and in Shrewsbury in 1519, where hops were labeled a "wicked and pernicious weed." As late as 1545, Andrew Boorde would write in his treatise on dietary health that unhopped ale was the natural drink of an Englishman, while hopped beer,† which made men bloated and fat, was better for Dutchmen—by which he meant uncouth Continentals. For the fifteenth and a sizable chunk of the sixteenth century, hopped "beer," as it came to be known, was looked

---

*Any monastic brewing that did take place in England, or Ireland for that matter, would have come to a screeching halt under the Dissolution of the Monasteries enacted by King Henry VIII. Alas, Trappist ales would have to be confined to the Catholic corners of northern Europe—which seems to have worked out pretty well for Belgium.

†It's worth noting that the nomenclature can be a bit confusing. Essentially, the words *ale* and *beer* have changed meaning over the years. Today, as we'll soon see, they can connote two different kinds of yeast, used in ales and lagers respectively. Originally, however, the terms simply indicated whether or not a brew was hopped.

The preservative properties of hops improved batch consistency and helped prevent spoilage. What had been a drink to be consumed locally and quickly became a commercial product capable of being casked and shipped to more distant markets.

upon by English ale drinkers much the same way a die-hard Schlitz fan from Milwaukee might a six-pack of Zima—as something foreign, effete, and flat-out disgusting.

The English valiantly resisted the incursions of Continental hopped beer onto their ale-loving soil, but alas, as with the Normans several centuries before, it was an invasion they could not repel, and an arrival that would eventually prove necessary to the future of the industry. In fact, by the very end of the sixteenth century, they had actually developed a fondness for the stuff; hopped beer caught on, and unhopped, sweet-tasting ale slowly went the way of feudalism and jousting contests. In 1556, the remaining ale brewers of London were absorbed by beer brewers in an umbrella guild that included the former only as something of a historical curiosity. And by the 1570s, even the smallest beer brewers were producing more per year than the largest ale brewers. If any nails in the coffin were needed, they came by way of William Harrison, who wrote in 1577 that ale was "an old and sick man's drink," with waning popularity across the kingdom.

But the question remains: How did a country of ale drinkers become beer-loving hop-heads in less than a century? In short, the reason is quality control. With larger, more industrial breweries making ever-increasing quantities of beer, measures were required to ensure that each batch would come out the same (meaning no contamination by unwanted pathogens), and that it would last as it was transported to its many distribution outlets and sold across the city. And unhopped ale just wasn't reliable. A very early example of this is the celebrated case of the fourteenth-century alewife Mary Kempe:

> She took up brewing, and was one of the greatest brewers in the town . . . for three or four years until she lost a great deal of money, for she had never had any experience with that business. For however good her servants were and however knowledgeable in brewing, things would never go successfully for them. For when the ale had as fine a head of froth on it as anyone might see, suddenly the froth would go flat, and all the ale was lost in one

brewing after another, so that her servants were ashamed and would not stay with her.

Here we have the problem in a nutshell: an independent alewife from a provincial town attempting to brew at a larger quantity for profit, and failing because of poor batch consistency. The hops used at the bigger commercial breweries in East Anglian cities and towns were able to solve the conundrum; their antimicrobial properties kept batches from getting infected with uninvited germs, and allowed them to remain free of such contamination long enough to be sold.

The other significant argument for hops, beyond simple preservation, was one of efficiency. English ale brewers had historically used large amounts of malted grain to strengthen their drink, in the hopes that it would keep longer. But when hopped beer arrived in London, brought from the Continent by immigrant Dutch brewers in the wake of the Hundred Years' War, a less costly way to preserve beer came with it. Since beer brewers used hops to the same effect, less grain was needed. According to a treatise on hops written by Reginald Scot, "whereas you cannot make above 8 or 9 gallons of indifferent ale out of one bushel of malt, you may draw 18 or 20 gallons of very good beer." This is supported by a beer recipe from 1502, which states quite confidently that a brewer could draw sixty barrels of beer from ten quarters of malt—about twenty-seven gallons per bushel. That came out to roughly half as much grain to brew hopped beer as unhopped ale. This naturally manifested itself in price, and as early as the fifteenth century, the cost of supplying English soldiers stationed in France was thirty shillings for a tun of ale, versus less than fourteen shillings for a tun of beer. In an expanding market that relied heavily on distribution—which England in the 1500s unquestionably was—the brewing of perishable, inefficient ales simply made poor economic sense. By the end of the century, London could boast some twenty successful breweries, positioned strategically along the Thames, churning out over one million gallons of high-quality, long-lasting, hopped English beer.

All of which sets the stage rather nicely for a trip aboard the *Mayflower*. Because as it turns out, hops wasn't the only controversial idea that leapfrogged the English Channel and settled in East Anglia in the sixteenth century, as indicated by this little period ditty:

> *Hops, Reformation, Bays and Beer*
> *Came to England in one bad year.*

Indeed, *the* Reformation, led by the French theologian John Calvin, made its way to England around the same time hopped beer was beginning to catch on. There were some adherents—nonseparating Puritans—who advocated for change from within the Church of England. But there were others—the more radical Separatists—who saw their differences as irreconcilable, and sought, as their name implies, a total separation and a new beginning. And the folks we've come to know here in America as the Pilgrims were unquestionably the latter. It should go without saying that the distaste was mutual; fines and prison sentences were imposed upon those who did not attend Church of England services. The Pilgrim chronicler William Bradford explains:

> But after these things they could no longer continue in any peaceable condition, but were hunted and persecuted on every side, so as their former afflictions were but as flea-bites in comparison of these which now came upon them. For some were taken and clapt up in prison,

others had their houses beset and watcht night and day, and hardly escaped their hands; and the most were faine to flie and leave their howses and habitations, and the means of their livelehood.

A hard-knock life indeed for the predecessors of the Pilgrims, and when those fines and sentences began to mount, and circumstances became completely unbearable, they did what most would do in their position: they skipped town. And like any Englishman of that era, they took their fondness for taverns and thirst for English beer with them. After all, they did quite literally drink the stuff like water.

The pickings were slim in old Europe when it came to finding a new home—especially after a sojourn in Holland didn't work out. But across the Atlantic, there were two entire continents to choose from. Guiana was proposed as a possible destination, but its climate was ultimately deemed too foreign, too hot. Virginia was another option, but that seemed a little too close for comfort to the king—the young colony was still governed by English law. The obvious solution? Found a colony of their very own. It took some finagling, and no small amount of intervention from well-connected friends, but land patents were secured and a plan was made: the Pilgrims would found a new plantation north of the nascent colony of Virginia, to be called New England.

On September 16, 1620, the *Mayflower* set sail, with just over one hundred passengers, and a hold laden with small beer—the low-alcohol brew preferred by Englishmen. Given the preservative properties of the hops, beer on voyages was far superior to water, which, if it wasn't polluted to begin with, often turned brackish. But even with a considerable beer supply, there were still problems. Strong storms halfway through the trip not only blew them off course and sent them farther north than intended, they also damaged the ship and slowed her progress, leaving the passengers low on rations and vulnerable to illness. When the *Mayflower* at last limped into Plymouth Harbor, the passengers and the crew were desperate for food and beer. As William Bradford recounted, lack of beer was one of the key reasons the Pilgrims decided to drop anchor:

> So in the morning, after we had called on God for direction, we came to this resolution—to go presently ashore again and to take a better view of two places which we thought most fitting for us; for we could not now take much time for further search or consideration, our victuals being much spent, especially our beer, and it now being the nineteenth of December.

Indeed, the beer shortage was a source of stress for all aboard the *Mayflower*. Tensions had escalated considerably between the passengers and the crew because of it. The captain, a man named Christopher Jones, was concerned he would not have enough for his men on the voyage back. Eager to get rid of the beer-glugging Pilgrims, he had no qualms about giving them the boot. "When this calamity fell among the passengers who were to be left here to settle," Bradford writes, "they were hurried ashore and made to drink water, so that the sailors might have more beer and when one sufferer in his sickness desired but a small can of beer, it was answered that if he were their own father he should have none." But the captain's selfish attempt to save his own hide proved ill-conceived. When the same sickness that had enfeebled the malnourished Pilgrims spread to him and his men, he realized they would not be able to make the voyage back to England until they were fully recovered and restocked. Understanding at last that they were quite literally all in the same boat, he had a change of heart. He became "somewhat struck," and "sent to the sick ashore and told the Governor that he could send for beer for those who had need of it, even should he have to drink water on the homeward voyage." Needless to say, it was probably not the most upbeat beer run in the history of New England, but those few extra calories from Captain Jones's private beer stash very likely saved the day. It was beer that dropped the Pilgrims in Plymouth, and beer, as it turns out, that allowed them to persevere.

The remaining stock of *Mayflower* beer didn't last long, and although a brewhouse was among the Pilgrims' very first projects, one can only surmise, based on the raw desperation of those first few years, that little if any beer was made. Only half of the original colonists survived that first trying New England winter, and it was only thanks to a little help from the region's Native Americans that anyone survived it at all. The English grains the Pilgrims attempted to plant failed miserably; the meager six acres of barley, from which English beer had traditionally been made, was only "indifferent good," and the peas "not worth gathering." Corn, however, introduced to the Pilgrims by a sympathetic Wampanoag known to history as Squanto, did grow, and it was because of this New World grain that the Plymouth Colony was able to persevere. And while corn can indeed be made into beer, and certainly was by many indigenous peoples of North and South America, Pilgrim testimonies from the early years of the Plymouth Colony make it clear water had temporarily replaced beer as the everyday drink:

> For the Countrey it is as well watered as any land under the Sunne, ever family, or every two families having a spring of sweet waters betwixt them, which is farre different from the

waters of England, being not so sharpe, but of a fatter substance, and of a more jetty colour; it is thought there can be
no better water in the world, yet dare I not preferred it before
good Beere, as some have done, but any man will choose it
before bad Beere, Wheay, or Buttermilke. Those that drinke
it be as healthful, fresh, and lustie, as they that drinke beere.

As good Englishmen, the Pilgrims may have suffered an initial
shock at having to drink water instead of beer, but they were also
quick to adapt. Fortunately for them, beer was coming soon. By
the late 1620s, the Pilgrim fathers had finally figured out how to
grow barley in New England; the fast-ripening grain does best
when planted in cool ground just above freezing, and given the
harshness of Massachusetts winters and heat of its summers,
farmers surely adjusted their traditional English planting schedule
to suit the severity of the new climate. In 1628, to complement the
increase in grain production, the first shipload of cultivated hops
arrived in Massachusetts via the Endicott Fleet.

Fast on the heels of those early Puritan trailblazers, a fresh wave
of better-prepared and better-provisioned immigrants was on its
way from the townships of East Anglia, with plenty of malt and
hops stowed away for the ride. In what would come to be known
as the Great Migration, some twenty thousand Puritans left their
cities and towns in southeastern England for the Plymouth and
Massachusetts Bay colonies between 1620 and 1640, bringing
their predilection for beer with them. In 1630, the ship *Arbella*
pulled into Boston Harbor with 10,000 gallons of beer and 120
hogsheads of malt. Just two years after that, under the governor-
ship of John Winthrop, the Massachusetts Bay Colony was already malting its own grains on an industrial scale to supplement
imports, and by 1634, Samuel Cole had established "Cole's Inn,"
a licensed tavern that served beer and very likely brewed it as well,
directly across from Governor Winthrop's house. It's a safe bet

When the Winthrop Fleet came to New England in 1630, it didn't just bring hundreds of eager Puritans fleeing religious prosecution—it brought enough malt and barley to get the taps flowing again.

the good governor was not above stopping in for a pint. Stronger wine and distilled spirits may have been looked upon with a Puritan's grim suspicion, but their beer—dark and cloudy due to its fire-roasted malts and top-fermenting yeast, oaky and tart thanks to time spent in the cask—was regarded in New England, just as it had been in Old England, as something both delicious and indispensable, a necessity and a joy.

Not only did the drinking trends of southeastern England make the trip across the water, older traditions were born anew, in a society whose uncultivated hinterland and immature cities resembled more closely the English countryside of the Middle Ages than seventeenth-century London. As such, it may come as no surprise that some familiar friends made a comeback—one of whom was the alewife. Women by necessity once again took up brewing, and the art became, at least in rural areas, a quotidian domestic activity. The most famous New England alewife was Sister Bradish, who in the late seventeenth century was supplementing her baking income—just as provincial Englishwomen had done three centuries before—by brewing and selling her own beer. New England's own native son Increase Mather would write of her: "Such is her art, way, and skill that shee doth vend such comfortable penniworths [of beer] for the relief of all that send unto her as elsewhere they can seldom meet with." This was in Cambridge, mind you, evidence that even right outside of an urban center like Boston, it was still challenging to find a decent commercially produced beer.

The Pilgrims also returned to the Old English habit of using flavoring agents and ingredients other than hops and barley. This wasn't a matter of preference, but once again, a question of necessity—hops shortages were common in seventeenth-century New England and would continue well into the eighteenth century as well. On occasion, even barley became scarce, or at the very least too scarce to brew with. Accordingly, early New Englanders sought other methods, just as their predecessors had back on the other side of the sea. One option was to use corn—a practice John Winthrop's own son had tinkered with in Connecticut during the mid-seventeenth century, earning him membership to the Royal Society of London. Oats, wheat, and rye were sometimes incorporated, and when all else failed, the Puritans could rely on some rather unusual ingredients to fill in the gaps. A common verse from the period sums it up rather nicely:

> If barley be wanting to make into malt,
> We must be content and think it no fault,
> For we can make liquor to sweeten our lips,
> Of pumpkins, and parsnips, and walnut-tree chips.

Here's evidence of just how far back those pumpkin-flavored fall microbrews really go. And when there was barley but a lack of hops, spruce was the most common flavoring agent thrown into the mix. Early colonists quickly learned, thanks again to a little Yankee ingenuity, that the fresh shoots of the black or red American spruce could be boiled to an essence and used as a replacement for both Old World cultivated hops and the wild American hops that could be sometimes found growing in the forest. So prominent was the practice of "sprucing" beer, it would become a treasured part of New England folk culture for some time to come. While you're not likely today to see any "Spruce Light" on tap at your local Southie pub, it was for much of the colonial era one of the most prominent regional beers in America, appearing in cookbooks and brewing manuals well into the 1800s.

As the first scattering of New England settlements transformed into New England cities over the course of the seventeenth century, it was only natural that the most beloved English beer tradition of all would take a firm hold: the tavern. The making and serving of beer became a crucial part of urban professional life, as tradesmen and merchants sought out a place to relax and discuss the issues of the day. Commonly referred to as an "Ordinary," the New England version of the old English tavern quickly became a fixture of life in the region's towns and cities. Soon after Samuel Cole opened "Cole's Inn" in 1634, Fairbanks Tavern broke ground between State and Water Streets in Boston, becoming a crucial gathering place for the community.* Stephen Hopkins and Francis Sprague followed suit with their drinking establishments in nearby Plymouth, and in 1636, a deacon named Thomas Chisholm even opened a tavern attached to

---

*Interestingly, the first overseas mail was received at the tavern in 1639, making it America's first post office. Messages and letters were attached to a "post" at the entrance.

his own church in Cambridge—a convenient way, no doubt, to spread the holy "spirit."

Taverns and inns appeared in Watertown, Salem, Charlestown, and Dorchester and quickly spread beyond the colonies of Massachusetts. We know Rhode Island had laws in effect to restrict tavern operations on Sundays by 1647, by encouraging men to practice with a bow and arrow rather than drink, with the former deemed "both man-like and profitable." In 1644, Connecticut towns were required to have at least one tavern, and in 1667, Maine received its first tavern in the form of a boozy ferry terminal in Kennebunkport. Back in Boston, by the late seventeenth century, the drinking scene had exploded, turning it into the tavern capital of New England. In 1673, Boston could claim twenty licensed taverns; four years later, that number had climbed to nearly thirty, and by the 1680s, there were dozens.* Men generally sat at benches after being served from behind a barred dispensary, and it was customary for newcomers to announce their name, profession, and hometown upon entering the establishment—an old New England habit that Benjamin Franklin would keep alive, even down in Philly, well into his old age. Some would serve imported wine and *aquavitae* (hard liquor), others allowed pipe smoking and the playing of bar games, and a few even doubled as courthouses and debate societies. But the one thing they all had in common was that they all served beer, and in many cases, brewed it themselves right on the premises.

It wasn't only New England taverns that served up Puritan beer. The old English trade practice of beer rationing at workplaces and institutions lived on in towns and cities across the region. In 1638, a typical ration for a sailing ship's crew

---

*It's worth noting that Boston's modern Bull Lane, Black Horse Lane, Red Lion Lane, and Cross Street were all originally named after the colonial taverns that once stood there—not bad legacies for humble colonial pubs.

in New England was a quart of beer per day, while a colonial cook by the name of Richard Briggs went so far as to demand workers be served only the finest beer while on the clock, stating that if poor-quality beer was served, "the drinkers of it will be feeble in summer time, incapable of strong work, and will be subject to distempers." Even more highbrow workplaces practiced a healthy dose of daytime drinking. As an older man, Benjamin Franklin would fondly recall his beer-drinking days down at the printing press as such:

> We had an alehouse boy who attended always in the house to supply the workmen. My companion at the press drank everyday a pint before breakfast, a pint at breakfast with his bread and cheese, a pint between breakfast and dinner, a pint at dinner, a pint in the afternoon about six o'clock, and another pint when he had done his day's work.

You needn't be an accountant to realize this adds up to quite a few pints over the course of a workday, or an HR rep to see that drinking beer was as much a part of office life in early New England as PowerPoint and Excel charts are today.

And speaking of highbrow establishments, no report on New England beer rationing would be complete without detailing the tumultuous brew history of that small liberal arts school Harvard University. Education was important to Puritans—they saw literacy and theology as crucial components of understanding the Bible—and establishing a place of higher learning was among their first priorities. "New College," as it was first known, was formed in 1636 by the Massachusetts Bay Colony, with beer playing an important role from the start. According to legend (and some admittedly circumstantial evidence), the institution's initial benefactor and later namesake, the Puritan minister John Harvard, learned the art of brewing back in England from William Shakespeare himself. The claim may be dubious, but there is no denying the founder of New England's premier institution of higher learning had beer in his blood; his father Robert Harvard had been a tavern keeper in Southwark, England.

Unfortunately, Harvard the younger died early into his involvement with the fledgling university. The headmaster left in charge, Nathaniel Eaton, did not share John's deep appreciation for the importance of beer and mismanaged its supply with disastrous results. While the newly named Harvard College could boast North America's very first printing press by 1638, its students were in open revolt just one year later thanks to severe shortages of their staple drink, complaining that "they often had to go without their beer and bread." That the university's first president liked to whip the college's students and tutors for fun didn't help either.* Finally, the stingy and mean-tempered Eaton got the boot, and the beer situation improved dramatically. A new president, Henry Dunster, was appointed in 1640, and although a strict man, he made sure both ale and beer were served in the main hall with meals (tobacco, though, he preferred to be used "in private"). Under his leadership, the school constructed its own brewery—Dunster thought it better that students drink beer on campus than stronger wine and spirits at nearby taverns—and by 1667, rules were put in place to ensure the Harvard brewery was producing both small and strong beer for the students to drink. The provisions dictating a healthy ration of beer for all students

---

*Many students also complained that their headmaster's wife had served them hasty pudding with goat dung in it, which should make modern students think twice before griping about dining hall fare.

would stay on the books through most of the eighteenth century, and if word around the finals clubs is to be believed, the drink is still enjoyed by Harvard students to this very day—part of a beer-guzzling New England collegiate tradition dating back almost four centuries.

As one can imagine, so much general beer drinking in New England society naturally caused concern among the Puritan elders—gentlemen who weren't known for kicking back and letting down their hair. While few would deny that small beer in small quantities was a daily necessity, they did not approve in the least of overindulgence and intoxication.* And with the rise of taverns and workplace drinking, penalties for alcohol abuse were soon to follow. As early as 1637, the Massachusetts General Court was concerned about the amount of time colonists were spending in the "ordinaries," and demanded nothing stronger was to be sold than weak penny beer. Tavern keepers were also ordered not to sell alcohol after nine o'clock on weekdays and forbidden to serve any customer who shirked his midweek church duties—early blue laws designed to keep order.

Predictably, these laws didn't do much to curb problem drinking. The very next year in Plymouth, following a fresh batch of intoxication fines, a Mr. William Reynolds was "presented for being drunck at Mr. Hopkins house, that he lay under the table, vomiting in a beastly manner." He was fortunate and only fined six shillings. His neighbor Mathew Southerland was not so lucky—he had to spend time in the stocks for his binge drinking. Corporal punishment was often implemented to punish piss-drunk Pilgrims, and while a first and second offense usually resulted in a fine, third

---

*There was one exception, though, and that was funerals. Those were the only occasions when drunkenness was not only accepted by Puritans, it was actually encouraged. Even children were allowed to get drunk.

offenses generally carried with them time in the stocks or whippings. A visiting Dutchman commented on New Englanders: "Whoever drinks himself drunk they tie to a post and whip him, as they do thieves in Holland." As to what constituted the legal definition of drunkenness, the Puritan version of a roadside sobriety test was as follows: the drunk was he who "either lisps or falters in his speech by reason of much drink, or that staggers in his going, or that vomits by reason of excessive drinking, or cannot follow his calling." In their efforts to curb tavern drunkenness, Puritan elders tried everything, from outlawing dancing to forbidding smoking; in 1643, they even banned shuffleboard, dragging the games from every tavern that offered it. None of it worked. From the get-go, it seems, New Englanders just liked to drink.

The first few generations of colonists were essentially transplanted middle-class English burghers from East Anglia imbibing in the New World just as they had in the Old. The same hopped beer, the same welcoming taverns, the same daily consumption and rationing as a staple. And in a wider historical context, these early-seventeenth-century Puritans, though at odds with the sanctioned church of their homeland, still thought of themselves fundamentally as English. The process of creating a uniquely American and regional identity would take time, but it did happen; through their interactions with their environment and climate and indigenous neighbors, a fresh idea began to take hold: they were Yankees, the New World progeny of a distant land—a country that faded further each year from living memory. And as we know all too well, friction between the emerging colonial identity and the English Crown was not far behind. The Puritans may have escaped the influence of the king and his church, but they were in no way exempt from English law and economic policy—even when they ceased to consider themselves English, or Puritans, for that matter. As more and more laws were passed back in London that favored the Old Country at the expense of the New, American habits were affected accordingly.

And drinking was no exception. Throughout the 1600s, beer had been *the* table beverage of all New Englanders, except for those trying first years when they were forced to drink water. But by the beginning of the eighteenth century, this was shifting—not due to changes in taste, but rather economic necessity. Mother England, who had colonies not just in New England, but throughout the Caribbean and the American South as well, needed surplus Yankee grain to feed its sugar and tobacco-producing plantations. New England grain production was highly regulated and taxed as a result. Grain shortages ensued (and subsequent hop shortages as well), and what barley, corn, and wheat was available came at a far steeper price.

So New Englanders began to look elsewhere for a reliable, mildly alcoholic beverage to take with their daily meals. And what did they drink when beer got too pricey? Cider, the fermented juice of the humble apple. Not that beer was no longer consumed—it was, especially in urban areas with easy access to imported malt and foreign brews. But particularly in small towns and on farms, it made little sense to make a drink from valuable grain, when fermentable apples could be had for next to nothing. The fruit trees, first brought to America by the Bostonian preacher William Blaxton in 1625, thrived in the New England soil and climate. It took the rest of that century for them to propagate and spread throughout the region, but by the late 1600s and early 1700s, apple orchards were so plentiful, the fruit was virtually free for the taking—most farms produced more apples than they could sell or consume.

The natural solution was to ferment the excess and drink it right up. By the mid-1700s, some New England families were consuming as much as a barrel of cider each week; in the year 1771, Middlesex County, Massachusetts, alone produced 22,780 barrels of the drink. Taking into account the total population was only 14,028, this comes out to a barrel and a half for every man, woman, and child. At the King's Head Tavern in Boston—owned by James Pitson for most of the first half of the eighteenth century—hundreds of barrels of cider were generally kept on hand, compared to only a few dozen bottles of beer. As the eighteenth century unfolded, cider came to challenge, and in many cases take over, beer's role as the favored table drink of New England. Even a die-hard patriot like John Adams loved cider—he drank a tankard of it every morning before breakfast.

New England beer also found a colonial rival in the form of rum. With the explosive growth of Caribbean sugar production in the late-seventeenth and early-eighteenth centuries—much of it on islands owned by the British—there was suddenly a glut of inexpensive molasses. And the British, who were never lacking when it came to exploiting their colonies for financial gain, realized almost immediately that the New England colonies were the perfect place to dump it. New England's first rum distillery appeared in 1648; by 1717, there were twenty-seven of them in Boston alone, and a decade later, that number had increased to forty. By the 1770s, the English colonies in America had some 140 molasses distilleries, making more than five million gallons of rum on their own, to augment another four million gallons being imported from the Caribbean. Whereas the Massachusetts Bay Colony had fined colonists for daring to brew with cheaper molasses in 1667, by the mid-1700s, spirits and brews made from molasses had become standard fare across New England.

Sam Adams wasn't just a patriot and founding father—he came from a long family tradition of farming and malting barley for the beer industry.

British mercantilist policies may have turned the region into a colony of cider freaks and rummies, but that doesn't mean everyone was content with the status quo. Not one bit, as a matter of fact. As early as 1711—more than sixty years before the Boston Tea Party—Bostonians were rioting down

Taverns like the Green Dragon provided a safe haven for patriots, a place where they could trade rounds *and* ideas for besting the British. These establishments were direct descendants of the alehouses of East Anglia, where the first Puritans had also gathered to voice their dislike of the English Crown.

by the harbor during a barley and wheat shortage and preventing the appropriately named merchant Andrew Belcher from sending off a shipload of the precious grain. The price of both bread and beer had inflated to unsustainable levels thanks to the hoarding of New England merchants like Belcher, who made a fortune selling local grain to British interests in the Caribbean, and the good people of Boston replied in kind by sawing off his rudder and raiding his warehouses. At Yale College over in New Haven, students were already eschewing British-controlled rum by 1764, insisting that "all gentlemen of taste who visit the College will think themselves better entertained with a glass of good beer." And over the decade that followed, those first rumblings of discontent were fermenting into a genuine notion that perhaps New Englanders—indeed, Americans—would be better off severing ties with old King George completely. In 1765, the *Boston Gazette* published the following screed against British policies that prevented Americans from becoming self-reliant:

> A colonist cannot make a button, a horseshoe, nor a hobnail, but some snooty ironmonger or respectable buttonmaker of England shall bawl and squall that his honor's worship is most egregiously maltreated, injured, cheated, and robbed by the rascally American republicans.

That same year, a group calling itself "the Sons of Liberty" began orchestrating effigy burnings and acts of vandalism to protest the passing of the unpopular Stamp Act and decry publicly the injustices of taxation without representation. A booze importer and beer lover by the name of John Hancock had no qualms voicing his disdain when the British confiscated his sloop *Liberty* in 1768 and charged him with smuggling for failing to pay duties. He was fed up with the high taxes and heavy-handed trade policies of Mother England, as were a growing number of his compatriots. This wasn't just about taxes on booze; it was the beginning of a national call to arms. Following the Boston Massacre of 1770 and the Tea Act of 1773, the call became all the more pressing. When it came to planning the first stages of an open rebellion, however, there was only one place where a gathering of disgruntled colonials wouldn't arouse undue suspicion: the local tavern. Clandestine meetings were held in establishments like Boston's storied Green Dragon—ones not so very different from the secret gatherings rebellious Puritans once held in the taverns of East Anglia.

Hancock's colonial associates rallied to his cause. Among them was the barley farmer, hereditary maltster, and latter-day namesake for one of New England's most well-known brews, none other than Mr. Samuel Adams himself—the very man whose face (or at least some artist's rendering of such) is staring at me proudly from the bottle of Boston Lager I just pulled from the fridge. As to whether or not he was actually much of a brewer is a matter of long-standing debate, but there's no denying that he and his drinking buddies helped start a revolution.

CHAPTER 2

❧

NEW YORK AND THE MID-ATLANTIC

or

Of Yankee Clippers

and Flying Dutchmen

SEVENTY-FIVE DEGREES FAHRENHEIT, NOT A CLOUD IN the sky at Yankee Stadium. Fine weather indeed for watching baseball—and, as it just so happens, for drinking beer. Although I must confess, my motives for being here are more directly related to the latter. Not that I don't love baseball, or the Yankees for that matter. I do, despite some lingering resentment left over from a childhood spent rooting for the Cleveland Indians. But I am here today primarily to check out the beer selection. According to the *Washington Post*, the Yankees have one of the worst beer selections in the game. A bold claim, I thought, and one that warranted further investigation. As soon as the seventh-inning stretch comes, I go for a beer run, quietly mouthing the lyrics to "Take Me Out to the Ball Game" as I attempt not to fantail too many people on my way down the aisle.

I shimmy down the row of seats and make my way up the austere concrete stairs, arriving at the concessions mildly out of breath and surprisingly thirsty. There's a substantial line ahead of me, which gives me plenty of time to examine my options. And honestly, they aren't *that* bad. To be sure, there are the more pedestrian brews, the Heineken and the Coors, but there's also Goose Island, Guinness, Magic Hat, Smithwick's. Perhaps the selection is not quite up to par with the Padres, who, according to the article, have eleven beers with scores of at least 90 on *Beer Advocate*. Or Seattle, where top-notch craft brews like Rogue and Pyramid outsell regular domestics by four-to-one. But then again, it's not quite the Cleveland Municipal Stadium I remember from my youth either, where the choices were limited to "ice-cold Budweiser" or "ice-cold Bud Light." We've become a more epicurean nation in the last few decades, and the times, they are indeed a-changing. Not that I'm complaining at all—it's really just the nostalgia talking, the old cant of the beer vendors making their way through the bleachers, crunching over peanut shells and singing out their wares.

There is, however, a certain serendipity to all this Yankee beer hubbub, since the team itself was built on beer. Knicker-bocker beer, to be exact, a now-defunct brand owned by the great New York beer baron Jacob Ruppert. It was Ruppert who bought the franchise in 1915, brought the great Babe Ruth to the Big Apple, and turned the team into the power-house it still is today. All with beer money, mind you. And it's fitting that Ruppert's brand was called Knickerbocker. An Anglicization of the Dutch surname *Knikkerbakker,* the word had become a playful moniker for the first settlers who came to New Netherland. While Knickerbocker beer was a favor-ite of the city's German American contingency by the early 1900s, the tradition of large-scale, entrepreneurial brewing it represented went directly back to the earliest days of the former colony. Unlike New England, which was first settled by religious separatists looking to found their own Puritan society, New Netherland was established by open-minded Dutch merchants seeking to make a savvy buck. They brought the values of tolerance, entrepreneurship, and diversified commerce from the ports of Old Amsterdam, directly to the streets of New Amsterdam—a scrappy little settlement on the southern tip of an island that the local Lenape people referred to as "Manna-hata." Oh, and beer. The Dutch brought that to New York, too.

"Next!" a frazzled-looking young man shouts from behind the tap. Snapped from my historical stupor, I realize I've come to the front of the line. I examine my options and consider my choices, but this is a baseball game, after all, and all the organic hops in the world have got nothing on childhood nostalgia.

"I'll have an ice-cold Bud," I tell the young man, just as the mounting roar behind me announces that the New York Yankees have taken the lead.

Had the Pilgrims' compasses proved more accurate, and had a storm not blown the *Mayflower* way off course, New York City may have been settled first by Puritanical Englishmen rather than free-wheeling Dutchmen. The mouth of the Hudson was, after all, the ship's intended destination. Luckily for those who appreciate Manhattan's cosmopolitan sophistication, towering skyscrapers, and rich bevvy of old Dutch names—Gansevoort, Brooklyn, Stuyvesant, and yes, even Coney Island—this was not the case. For while it was religion and self-determination that brought those first East Anglians to the shores of Massachusetts, the first Dutch settlers were brought to America by . . .

Hats.

Yes, hats. Beaver hats, more accurately. They were the rage in Europe at the time, thanks to their water resistance and incomparable warmth. And across the Atlantic in the wilderness of the New World, beavers abounded. What an ambitious trapper couldn't catch himself, he could easily purchase from Native Americans with beads, metal, or alcohol. A fair trade, perhaps not, but with European powers vying for control of international trade routes and colonial domination, these were hardly considerate times.

The Dutch colonial experiment in America began in earnest in 1609. In that year the Dutch East India Company in Amsterdam commissioned an upstart captain named Henry Hudson to poke around the New World and see if he couldn't find the fabled Northwest Passage to Asia. He did not, but he did discover lands rich in beaver, considerably farther north than that shabby little English settlement in Jamestown. Word spread, more Dutch ships followed, and by 1612, "New Amsterdam," as New York was first called, already had an infant settlement on the southern tip of Manhattan—not to mention a brewery, erected that same year by a couple of pioneers named Adrian Block and Hans Christiansen. An early start, indeed, for both New York City and New York–style beer.

The Dutch loved beer, as they had since very early times. Hailing from the same northern Germanic culture that had birthed the Angles and the Saxons, the Dutch also inherited a lusty taste for a brew. The mashing of grains into a drinkable beverage in the Low Countries is no doubt a very old phenomenon, although some of the earliest concrete archaeological evidence points to brewing taking place in the vicinity of Namur as early as the third and fourth centuries A.D.—just after the previous Roman occupants had begun abandoning their northern outposts and turning tail for the south. The Franks, another Germanic tribe, swept into the vacuum the fleeing Romans had left behind, to incorporate modern-day Holland—not to mention Belgium and northern France—into what would eventually become their Holy Roman Empire. With the propagation of Christianity in the seventh and eighth centuries, monasteries took root, and with them, a sudden need for large-scale brewing. After all, each local monastery had to produce enough beer for all the monks, not to mention the surrounding peasants, many of whom were still unconvinced as to the merits of churchgoing. Delicious beer, it turned out, was not a bad way to convince them.

By the twelfth and thirteenth centuries, monastic brewing was already a common feature of Dutch life. The monks brewed beer with a combination of popular flavoring spices called *gruit,* discovering along the way how to increase their profits. The abbey of St. Trond in the southern Low Countries was already taxing any rival brewers operating on their lands as early as 1112, by making them supply the monks with a weekly ration of ale. By 1141, the Crepin monastery had begun taxing independently brewed beer directly, using such funds to fill its own purse. And by the 1200s, Dutch municipalities just to the north had learned from the monks and gotten in on the game. The first Dutch town to engage in beer taxation was Haarlem, passing the excise in 1274; Leiden had brewing taxes of its own less than a century later. Slowly, beer production was shifting, from a rural and sacred activity to an urban and secular industry.

The Dutch had gotten a head start on the mass urbanization that spread across Europe during the Middle Ages. Large population growth in the eleventh and twelfth centuries, coupled with a whole lot of dike building and land reclamation to accommodate it, had brought rural peasants into Dutch towns early on. Consequently, by the thirteenth century, the Low Countries were the most urbanized part of Northern Europe. With breweries becoming more efficient and professionalized, quality and salability both improved drastically. Wine had been the drink of the privileged class through much of the medieval period—the abundance of Dutch seaports meant they always had a few imported bottles at the ready. But by the late thirteenth century, hops and commercial production had created a delicious brew that could rival fermented grape juice in taste. What had previously been the beverage of farmers and

In much of medieval Europe, monasteries were the only institutions with the resources to brew on a larger scale. When the monks produced more beer than they could drink, they generally weren't above selling it to the locals—which helped establish beer as a commercial product.

tradesmen was quickly adopted by drinkers across all classes, nobles included. The records from a countess of Holland and Hainault give some indication of just how ubiquitous beer had become in the Low Countries in the early 1300s: according to ledgers, everyone in her court drank beer, and by 1319, they were chugging back thirteen barrels on average each week. In nearby Flanders, the wealthy were generally taking wine with their meals in the thirteenth century—a hundred years later, good-quality beer had replaced imported German and French wines as a table beverage. And while a good deal of the beer Dutchmen drank had been originally imported from the Hanseatic towns of northern Germany, the Count of Holland had a monopoly going on taxing the *gruit* spices that were once used to flavor German beer. By the early 1300s, that same count was taxing imports heavily to help bolster production of domestic hopped brew, as the older *gruit*-flavored beer, much like English ale two centuries later, slowly went by the wayside. Thanks to the expertise of professional urban brewers, local Dutch beer had become too profitable to ignore. The municipal government in Zeeland even attempted to establish a *Brouwershaven,* a portside brewers' colony whose sole purpose was to increase beer output. The plan fell through, but the governing bodies of the Low Countries learned their lesson early on: more domestic beer meant a broader tax base. And the domestic beer industry grew accordingly.

When hops rather than *gruit* entered the equation, a technique picked up from their neighbors in northern France and Germany, the durability and consistency of Dutch beer improved immensely—and the Dutch prospered because of it. By the end of the fourteenth century, the town of Delft was drawing as much as 25 percent of its income from taxes placed on hopped beer. With beer becoming a major source of wealth, municipal governments had a vested interest in fostering the industry, and in regulating it to ensure high standards and output. By 1391, encouraged no doubt by the high demand in nearby urban centers, hops were being grown in the countryside as a field crop, even replacing grain in some areas. And in the fields that did grow grain, much

Commercial brewing on the Continent may have started with the monasteries, but it didn't take long for secular entrepreneurs to get in on the action. With the growth of towns and cities, the locus of brewing power shifted from the monasteries in the countryside to the brewers' guilds in town.

of it was used for beer. Thanks to the mild Dutch climate, oats and wheat could be grown right alongside barley, and most beer recipes included a larger proportion of the first two grains than was common in other parts of Europe. It was a trick the Hanseatic brewers of northern Germany had used to stretch grain supplies and enhance smoothness, and the Dutch, as it turns out, were a quick study. The result was a lighter, softer, and more drinkable beer, made from ingredients that were easy to come by.

As for production, well, it exploded. It's likely that by the end of the fourteenth century, Gouda, Delft, and Haarlem—the three biggest brew centers in Holland—were already producing more than 11,000,000 liters a year. A century later, this number had climbed by almost a factor of ten, to over 100,000,000 liters. In 1367, Gouda alone had at least twenty-six breweries; by the late 1400s, the town had over a hundred and fifty breweries to its name. The production of so much beer created an exportable surplus, and soon Dutch beer, which kept well thanks to its hop content, was being shipped everywhere the Dutch conducted trade. By the year 1500, the good burghers of Gouda were drinking just 10 percent of the beer they produced; the rest, they were exporting. In total, they were sending outside their city walls some 15,000,000 liters per year.

By the beginning of the sixteenth century, beer in the Netherlands had become big business, second only to textiles in the Dutch economy. When it came to quality and cost, foreigners simply could not compete. Beer was shipped first to Friesland and Hamburg, then to markets farther afield in France, England (after all, it was the Dutch who introduced both hopped beer and industrial brewing to London), Norway, and other nations along the North Sea coast. Some healthy free market competition among Dutch brewers had increased quality levels to all-time highs, and the development of industrial-sized brewing facilities meant more beer than ever was being produced. In 1517, an Italian familiar with Dutch beer remarked: "The beer in these regions is better than in Germany and brewed in larger quantity." When it comes to beer, if you're beating out the Germans, you're probably doing something right. In 1514, the three main Dutch brewing centers—Gouda, Delft, and Haarlem—were only consuming 7 percent of the beer that they brewed. The rest was shipped all across Europe.

Dutch beer had become an industry. This wasn't just a way for a farmer to quench his thirst or an alewife to make a buck; beer was now the lifeblood of an entire economy. And it was a form of symbiosis that both the Dutch brewers and the Dutch government acknowledged and fostered. In Holland, religious officers, shipbuilders, nobles, and members of many trade guilds were generally considered tax-exempt when it came to beer, and they were often granted excise-free barrels. It is no coincidence these were considered some of the most important contributors to the Dutch economy; keeping them happy (and mildly intoxicated, for that matter) was crucial to the industry, and the society. When Dutch beer prospered, the Dutch people prospered—the folks in charge were prescient enough to realize the health of one was inextricably linked to the other.

This, in a nutshell, was the beer tradition the Dutch brought to "New Netherland," a region that included portions of modern-day New York, New Jersey, Delaware, and Pennsylvania—basically, what would become the Middle Colonies. The culture of New Amsterdam was a direct reflection of the culture they had known in Old Amsterdam across the sea. Back home, the Dutch had learned the benefits of tolerance, granting refugee status to groups like exiled Sephardic Jews, French Huguenots, and fugitive English Puritans. This wasn't just being a good neighbor—it was also good for trade. Because all newcomers knew they were welcome, the ports of the Netherlands became more cosmopolitan and diverse, and new foreign markets and trading routes blossomed.

Directly related, the Dutch also witnessed firsthand the full potential of market stimulation. Beginning with the Count of Holland, the Dutch had understood that government policies that encouraged local entrepreneurship, when paired with friendly foreign relations, would stimulate economic growth and exports as a whole. It was precisely these sorts of policies that had turned a quaint wooden shoe–wearing people into an international powerhouse in less than a century, and those same policies would give beer its first solid foothold in the New World.

From its onset, the Dutch colony of New Netherland fared considerably better than its English competition to the north and south. Perhaps this was because they came better prepared, or possibly because, in tolerant Dutch fashion, they attempted to trade with the local Indians rather than shout Bible verses at them and chase them with muskets. But either way, while the Pilgrims were shivering through their "Starving Time," and the Virginians were fending off Powhatan tomahawks, the New Netherlanders were sitting around their fireplaces and sipping good Dutch-style beer. In 1623, they established colonies at Albany and Camden, and by 1625, they were digging the first foundations of New Amsterdam. There is the story about the island of Manhattan being purchased by Peter Minuit from its original Native American inhabitants for twenty-four dollars worth of beads and trinkets, although most modern estimates put the amount closer to a thousand. In either case, it was a bargain, and the Dutch had plenty of money left over to get the brew kettles working.

As early as 1626, they were already well aware that all the ingredients they needed for brewing could be grown in the New World; one Dutchman remarked that they could "brew as good beer here as in our Fatherland, for good hops grow in the woods." In short order, the Dutch settlers in New

Early investments in maritime trade as well as beer production helped give the Dutch an edge when it came to establishing colonies in the New World. At its peak, New Netherland stretched from upstate New York all the way down to Delaware, with Dutch-style beer consumed throughout.

Amsterdam were farming "rye, barley, wheat, oats, and hops, which could be distilled into hard liquor or brewed into strong beer." Their beer was likely lighter and smoother than many brews of that time, thanks to the wheat and oats that surely complemented the barley—essentially making them true pioneers in the use of adjunct grains in American brewing. The Dutch West India Company was quick to get in on the action, building in 1632 the colony's first large-scale brewery on what came to be called "Brouwers Straet,"* with ample encouragement from the governor, Wouter van Twiller. The colony was not very large at this point—fewer than four hundred Dutchmen called New Amsterdam their home—but one thing they all needed was a steady supply of beer. Laws were passed that restricted home brewing, ensuring that the industry remained for the most part a commercial and taxable affair.

Not that there was no competition. The Dutch West India Company was the major beer producer, but other entrepreneurial settlers, brought to New Netherland by the patroon system of land grants, lobbied to receive their own commercial brewing licenses. Upon receiving his grant, Kiliaen van Rensselaer, a jeweler from Amsterdam, wrote, "as soon as there is a supply of grain on hand, I intend to erect a brewery to provide all of New Netherland with beer, for which purpose there is already a brew kettle there." He would eventually go on to supply beer for all the retail accounts of the Manor of Rensselaerwyck, ensuring that all in the vicinity of that land grant had ample beer. An independent brewer named Evert Pels van Steltyn also received a license to brew when he arrived on the ship *Houttuyn*

---

*Many residents of Manhattan may know Brewers Street by its modern name, Stone Street. There is at least one story that it received its name from the first cobblestones that were put in—to keep New Yorker's feet clean, as it turned out. The leftover water runoff from all the breweries often turned the thoroughfare into muck. The breweries may be all gone, but with the many bars and drinking establishments it boasts today, New Yorkers can count on other things to dirty their shoes on Stone Street.

in 1637 with several hundred bushels of malt. Another brewer, one Jean Labadie, was granted permission ten years later to build a brewery, on the condition he pay annually for this favor "six merchantable Beavers to the company." But the most famous of those early Dutch brewers was Rutger Jacobsen van Schoenderwoert—the first part of his name turned out to be much easier to remember than the latter, and so his decendants adopted the surname "Rutgers," eventually leanding the name to Rutgers University, the nation's eighth-oldest institution of higher learning. It all started in 1649 when he agreed to pay 450 guilders yearly to rent a patroon's brewery.

Rutger may have been one of the first New Amsterdam brewers whose name still carries some currency, but he was certainly not the last. A quick rundown of Manhattan's early brewing community reveals a host of names most contemporary New Yorkers will recognize and indicates just how entrepreneurial that initial cohort of Dutch brewers truly was. There was Oloff Stevenson van Cortlandt, who saw both his new and old breweries damaged in a flood. The merchant Jacob Kip became one of the settlement's first successful beer traders, and the three Bayard brothers, Nicholas, Peter, and Balthazar, all included brewing among their vast collection of business interests. Today, there are parks, bays, and streets bearing the surnames of these early Dutch brewers, and it's not because they went broke or thought small. Brewing proved to be a foundation upon which many of New York's first fortunes were built. Indeed, even the first successful American beer "brand" came courtesy of the Dutch brewers in New Amsterdam. In 1660, investors Isaac de Foreest, Joannes Verveelen, and Johannes de la Montagne all pooled their resources to get the Red Lion Brewery up and running. And so for the first time in our nation's history, Dutch Americans, doing their best to make it in the Big Apple, could do more than simply order "a beer." They could doff their beaver caps, pony up to the bar, and order beer with a proper name: *one nice cold Red Lion, please.*

The Dutch of New Netherland continued to drink beer heavily, just as they had in the Low Countries back home. In most cases, the drinking culture was sanguine and salubrious—the perfect example of which was a well-known outdoor drinking pavilion that existed by one of Albany's freshwater ponds in the seventeenth century. Unlike in the smoky taverns of New England, drinkers would even congregate at this pleasant Dutch beer garden on the Sabbath to buy rounds and trade tales, and both men and women of all ages were welcome. Actually, it was the aging mother of its owner who paid the establishment its highest compliments, describing it as:

> A delightful place . . . where we would be able to taste the beer of New Netherland, inasmuch as it was also a brewery. . . . On account of its being to some extent a pleasant spot, it was resorted to on Sundays by all sorts of revelers. . . . Our company immediately found some acquaintances there and joined them.

Reading this account, one can almost imagine a scene straight out of a Pieter Bruegel painting, of jolly Dutchmen toasting their tankards with beloved spouses upon their laps, as beer lovers from the Low Countries re-created their festive traditions an ocean away in New Netherland. And for any modern New Yorker who appreciates the fact that Manhattan bars stay open not just on Sundays, but until four in the morning as well, you can thank those early Dutchmen for establishing a long-standing tradition of permissive drinking laws.

It wasn't all kind nods and ninepins, though. Just like their English neighbors to the north, Dutch settlers sometimes got rowdy when the beer flowed too freely. One common problem, it seems, was *over*friendly drinking. In seventeenth-century Dutch culture, it was considered rude to turn down a drink when offered. And in an overabundance of camradarie, brawls did break out when rejections ensued. "If you will not drink with me," roared one Dirk Bratt of Albany at his friend Jan Gow, "you must fight me." And because many brewers and taverns were owned by friends, it was not uncommon for overenthusiastic drunkards to barge their way in. In 1654, a Seeger Cornelisz knocked in the door of Merten the brewer "in such a way that the hinges sprang out of the posts and the casings." Just for a drink of beer, mind you. A few years later, Jasper Abrahamzen, a sailmaker from Amsterdam, "committed great violence and opposition" at Rendel Huit's house, when Rendel's wife was unwilling or unable to tap a keg and pour him a beer. There were laws prohibiting such behavior, but penalties for drunken tomfoolery were far less severe than in the Puritan colonies of New England. Fines and apologies were more common than whippings and stocks, and in the case of misdealings, an excuse of drunkenness could often get a defendant off the hook. Strict laws were also in place prohibiting the sale of alcohol to Indians and some African slaves, although such regulations generally concerned stronger spirits such as gin and rum, as opposed to weaker drinks like wine and beer. Beer was served at feasts and gatherings, but it was seldom used in cross-cultural trade given its shorter shelf life and weaker alcohol levels. Practically speaking, it was considered more of a foodstuff than an intoxicant, but that didn't stop the Dutch settlers from overindulging whenever they could. None of which should be particularly surprising given the abundance of brewers that existed in New Netherland, serving up a bounty of Dutch-style beer.

That's not to say all those drinking the beer were actually Dutch. By the mid-seventeenth century, the colony was growing, and just like the original Amsterdam across the sea, it had become diverse, cosmopolitan, and open to export. With its convenient location between the colonies in Virginia and New England, and its bustling markets in furs and other trade goods, it turned into a major international port, where the many peoples of the world could gather to do business. Whereas the Puritan fathers in New England were chasing nonconformists into the wilderness—that is, after all, how Rhode Island got started—New Amsterdam welcomed diversity. As early as 1613, the nascent colony received its first immigrant from the Dominican Republic, when the Dutch dropped off Juan Rodriguez on Governors Island. In 1628, French-speaking Huguenots, no longer wanted in the Old Country, established the *L'Église française a la Nouvelle-Amsterdam*. And in 1654, the city received its first Jewish immigrants from the Portuguese colony of Brazil; the Dutch West India Company worked hard to ensure that they were accepted in the colony, well aware of the fact that a little tolerance could go a long way when it came to commerce. One director bragged to a visitor in 1646 that there were "men of eighteen different languages" living together on the streets of what would one day become New York City, proof that the Big Apple was a melting pot long before Lady Liberty or Ellis Island came into being.

Not surprisingly, all of that multilingual tongue wagging made the colony quite parched. The population of the city was never huge under the Dutch, but it was thirsty. In 1637, Governor Kieft estimated that the places where tobacco and beer were sold amounted to a full quarter of the establishments in New Amsterdam. A decade later, Domine Backer would tell the Classis of Amsterdam that the settlement could boast seventeen licensed taverns, not to mention seven more that sold alcohol under the table. So much beer was being produced to stock them, the surplus could even be sent abroad. As early as the 1640s, New Amsterdam was exporting locally brewed beer down south to Virginia, and later, to the newer Dutch colonies in what today is Delaware.

The establishment of new breweries outside Manhattan only served to further boost the colony's production. By 1650, Albany had its own brewery owned by Captain Volkest Janse Douw, and in New Amstel to the south, beer was being made in the Dutch fashion by 1661 thanks to a brewer named Adam Dortmans. Meanwhile, the prosperous Rutgers family, which had grown enough to produce America's first true beer barons, was churning out suds for all New Netherland. Beer business in the Dutch colonies was booming—so much so, that by the late seventeenth century, Dutch American beer was being exported and sold all along the Eastern Seaboard . . . to the point where some of the Dutch colony's competitors began to take notice.

Not least of whom were the English. They'd had a few hiccups when it came to getting their settlements in Virginia and New England off the ground, but by the mid-1600s, things were going well. It was surely frustrating to have that Dutch wedge between their most important American territories. And thus, in 1664, although war was not technically declared, the Duke of York sent four frigates to New Amsterdam's harbor, with the intention of wresting control of the entire New Netherland colony—a swath of land that stretched from upstate New York all the way south to Delaware.

The English had warships, armies, and powerful guns. As for the Dutch, they had . . . windmills. That, and some very good beer. They didn't stand a chance when it came to military might. At first, the feisty director-general, Peter Stuyvesant, wanted to put up a fight, but he quickly came to the conclusion that the Dutch colony wouldn't last a day against British

The Dutch were savvy when it came to establishing colonies, but they lacked the military strength to keep them. In the end, the Dutch governor Peter Stuyvesant had no choice but to hand New Amsterdam over to the English.

seapower. With a helpless sigh, he surrendered and, by signing the Twenty-Three Articles of Capitulation, gave the English full control of the colony and its most important city—soon to be renamed New York. The British took charge of things, and a fresh wave of English-speaking settlers began to pour in, changing the face of the city for good. But just like all those old Dutch names that could not be erased—Harlem, Bronx, Brooklyn, Bowery—a tradition of cosmopolitan diversity and a spirit of ambitious entrepreneurship were both in New York to stay.* Twenty years after the conquest, the official language

---

*It's interesting to note that while the Dutch language died out in New York City, it continued to be spoken in New York's hinterlands well into the twentieth century. One famous native New York Dutch speaker was the U.S. president Martin Van Buren. He is the only president to date whose first language was not English.

might have been English, but the belief in a quality-controlled and commercially minded brewing culture that was directly supported by the government remained, as attested to by this "Bill Concerning Brewers," passed on October 23, 1684:

> Bee It Enacted, By this Generall Assembly & the Authority of the Same that noe person whatsoever shall undertake the Calling or work of Brewing Bear for Sale; but only Such as are known to have Sufficient Skill or knowledge in the art or Mistry of a Brewer; and If any Master of a Shipp or Vessell or any other person whatsoever shall purchase or buy any Bear of any Brewer within this Government; which Bear Shall prove unwholesome and Useless for their Suply either through the Insufficiency of the Mault or brewing or bad Cask; the person wronged thereby Shall be and Is Inabled by Vertue of this Act to maintain an Action against the person or persons from whome the said Bear was Received; and to Recover his Just damages.

Brewing had become lucrative, professionalized, and regulated: "Big Beer" and "Big Business" were both in New York City to stay.

When the English took over the Dutch colonies of New Netherland, however, they inherited more than Manhattan and its environs. The Dutch domain in the New World had stretched south through what is today coastal Pennsylvania and Delaware, colonies they in turn had appropriated from Sweden. So when the English got in on the action, there was already a tradition of Dutch settlement—and brewing—in the Mid-Atlantic region. At least one brewery could be found in the settlement of Tinicum, just below what would become Philadelphia, prior to 1654. When the Englishman William Penn finally landed there in 1682, he found the Blue Anchor Inn ready to serve him a frothy beer. In 1685, he reported seven such establishments, "for the entertainment of strangers and workmen that are not housekeepers." And it is not terribly surprising that his Quaker-friendly new colony would build upon that existing New Netherland groundwork. Penn helped foster a society that bore more resemblance to the tolerant, trade-oriented society of the Dutch before him than the Puritan or plantation settlements in New England and Virginia. He worked hard to stay on good terms with the local Indians—he even gifted them, at least on one occasion, with a barrel of beer—and encouraged settlers of all faiths and nationalities to settle there. When the time came, he founded his own small brewery at the estate he built in Pennsbury, a short boat ride up the river from Philadelphia. In 1684, he would write to his friend and construction manager James Harrison: "I would have a Kitchen, two larders, a wash house & a room to iron in, a brew house & in it an oven for baking." The house was eventually torn down, but the brewhouse remained standing until 1864. Evidence, perhaps, of just how strong a brewing foundation the City of Brotherly Love was built upon.

The town's first capable brewer was most likely William Frampton. An English Quaker, he died just a few years after arriving in Philadelphia. But before departing, he laid the earliest bricks in Philadelphia's nascent brewing industry. Penn referred to him as an "able man, that has set up a large Brew House, in order to furnish the People with good Drink, both there and up and down the river." By 1696, there were as many as four "spacious malt-houses," with working breweries right alongside them, producing enough beer to export outside the city. A contemporary settler described Philadelphia beer as "equal in strength to that in London," and said it was "in more esteem than English Beer in Barbadoes and is sold for a higher Price there." Here we have not just an early mention of Philly's famous colonial beer—which was made very much in the dark, hoppy style of the English—but one of the first instances of American beer being shipped abroad. Other seminal Philadelphia breweries included the Morris brewery established in 1687, and that of Joshua Carpenter, who made so much money in brewing, he had become the second-richest inhabitant of the town by 1693. In Philadelphia, just like in New York, the city and its fortunes were growing at a heady rate thanks to an early emphasis on the brewing of beer.

At least until the eighteenth century, that is. Because just like New England to the north, brewing in the Mid-Atlantic region was vulnerable to external influences. Rum would never be quite as popular as in New England, where most of the distilleries could be found, and enough locally produced malted grain was generally available to ensure that beer was never eclipsed by cider, as was often the case in more rural northern areas. Nonetheless, the colonial policies of the English, together with the rising popularity of rum and cider, did their damage and cut into profits. In the year 1700, the New York Provincial Legislature found itself compelled to pass "an act for Incouraging the Brewing of Beer and making Malt within this province." Arbitrary capitalization aside, this evidences that by the beginning of the eighteenth century, the local brewing industry was beginning to suffer, as the British government imposed high taxes on locally produced beverages to create an unchallenged market for their own.

Despite the competition, beer continued to be brewed in both New York and Philly, to a far greater extent than the rum-distilling towns of New England. The tradition of brewing on a large, industrial scale was simply too entrenched in the former Dutch colonies—unlike in Massachusetts, where the beer had been brewed commercially, but generally on a smaller, less ambitious scale. Larger breweries had the resources to weather fluctuations in grain prices and sudden incursions of cheap rum. In New York, the Rutgers family kept churning out large quantities of beer from their brewery on Stone Street—the same cobblestone lane that the Dutch had called "Brewers Street" years before. That brewery would relocate numerous times over the century, but it would continue to supply the city with much of its beer. Malted beverages were still consumed by the masses, especially at large gatherings; in 1734, for instance, Governor William Cosby rewarded a local militia with "12 Barrels of Beer to be distributed among them to drink to their Majesties and Royal Healths." In 1766, though, with local sentiment beginning to turn against the health of said Majesty, the mood had changed considerably—but not the drink. Men speaking out against the king celebrated their defiance with a roasted ox and "twenty-five barrels of ale, which were dispensed freely as long as they lasted." New Yorkers of both Dutch and English descent were beginning to question their allegiances, if not their beverages.

Similar anti-English sentiments were echoed in Philadelphia. The city had grown into the brew capital of colonial America by the mid-eighteenth century, outpacing even New York when it came to the quality of its beer. The local porter had a well-earned reputation as the best around; extra-dark thanks to its heavily roasted malts, it was enjoyed everywhere on the Eastern Seaboard, and it competed directly with English exports—a fact that surely infuriated British interests, who lobbied aggressively for increased taxation of American-made products. In 1765, just a year before the anti-English rally in New York mentioned above, two Philadelphia brewers, Thomas Paschall and George Emlen, had had enough. They cosigned a formal complaint directed at English merchants, stating that as a result of their protectionist attitudes, the colonies were considering a total boycott of all British goods. Beer, it goes without saying, was foremost among them. In 1769, when a literal boatload of good English malt arrived at the port of Philadelphia from Yarmouth, England, the patriotic brewers of America received their first test in solidarity. The brewers and merchants of the city convened and decided to reject the cargo, stating that they would "not purchase any part of it, nor will they brew the same, or any part thereof, for any person whatsoever." Harsh words from an increasingly dissatisfied colonial people.

The Tea Act of 1773 further provoked the colonists' ire, but it seemed to bother the Bostonians far more than it did New Yorkers or Philadelphians, who greeted it not so much with outrage, but with definite annoyance. Their grumbling may have amounted to little more than that, had a skirmish not broken out on April 19, 1775, in a couple of New England towns called Lexington and Concord. It seemed that maltster Sam Adams and his liquor importer friend Hancock were no longer content to suffer the unfair taxes and regulations imposed by the British government. There was an open revolt going on, and suddenly American colonists weren't just boycotting the British—they were preparing to attack.

The Middle Colonies were initially uneasy with the idea of a war for independence. At the Second Continental Congress, held in Philadelphia's State House, they debated the matter thoroughly. But when the British general William Howe invaded New York and took control of the city in the summer of 1776, no more convincing was required. The Declaration of Independence was officially adopted, as every fireworks lover knows, on July 4, 1776. George Washington had already been named commander of the Continental

Army, and a beer ration put into place: every soldier fighting for America's independence was to receive "1 quart Spruce beer or cyder" per day. The allowance was welcomed by troops, but it was not to last, as war shortages inevitably ensued. By 1778, Philadelphians were complaining about the inflation, stating that the price of "Strong Beer or Ale is extravagantly high, and much in Demand." Some brewers, like New York's William D. Faulkner, used the war to their own advantage, selling beer first to Washington's troops at a rate of three or four barrels a week, then later to the occupying British—so much so that by 1776, he had to buy twenty pounds of hops just to keep up. A number of the big brewing families of the Middle Colonies—the Rutgers, the Morrises, and the Lispenards—were able to survive the war with their fortunes and their breweries intact. But others did not, as trade embargos and local grain shortages pushed many out of business. America prevailed, but her brewing industry was in shambles. The war had taken its toll.

But then, the darnedest thing. When peace was made on September 3, 1783, and those feisty American colonists suddenly realized they had a new country on their hands, they also had to figure out what to drink. British products like rum and imported beer weren't just déclassé, they were now flat-out difficult to find. Which meant that if Americans wanted to keep tipping the wrist, they were going to have to make a whole lot more of their own alcoholic beverages. With the British finally off their backs, and grain markets unregulated and expanding, the obvious solution was beer. Before the war, the New York alcohol distributor Gerard G. Beekman had ordered his beer from Halifax and Londonderry; the Philadelphia-based firm of John and Clement Biddle was bringing in Scots ale manufactured by the Cunningham family of Glasgow. When hostilities began, though, the foreign supply had been essentially cut off—a plan B was desperately needed. Samuel Adams, while rallying American brewers to the cause, may have said it best:

> It is to be hoped, that the Gentlemen of the Town will endeavour to bring our own [strong] beer into fashion again, by that most prevailing Motive, EXAMPLE, so that we may no longer be beholden to Foreigners for a Credible Liquor, which may be as successfully manufactured in this country.

The ever-patriotic and sensible Benjamin Franklin echoed those sentiments, stating, "as we raise more [grain] than the English West-India Islands can take off, and since we cannot now sell it to the foreign Islands, what can we do with our Overplus better, than turn it into Spirit, and thereby lessen the Demand for West-India Rum, which our Grain will not pay for?" Granted, Benjamin may have been referring to spirits, but the message was the same: imported rum was out of the picture, and British beer was almost totally off-limits. The day had arrived for American beer to retake its place at the helm.

The nascent American government did its part to replace "the Demon Rum" and get the beer taps flowing again. Congressman James Madison led the charge when he "moved to lay an impost of eight cents on all beer imported . . . as to induce the manufacture to take deep root in every state in the Union." The first secretary of the Treasury, Alexander Hamilton, seconded that notion, stating in 1791, "It is desirable, and in all likelihood, attainable, that the whole consumption [of malt liquors] should be supplied by ourselves." At a local level, Massachusetts was among the first states to pass favorable brewing legislation, and New York, Pennsylvania, and New

Jersey all followed suit. And it worked. By 1794, one observer noted "the success of the Americans in the manufacture of malt liquors," and stated that "breweries are multiplying: as their value is becoming manifest." The rural commentator J. B. Bordley would remark that thanks to local brewing, "beer is taking the place of diluted spirits . . . there is more sobriety now observed in the towns than formerly, when West India rum abounded at a third of its present price."

In New York, families who had never touched a brew kettle before suddenly wanted in on the action. An entrepreneur named John Herring Sr., who apparently had no prior experience in the brewing industry, was confident he could "produce ale and porter of a quality superior to any sold in New York, at that time." So successful did his brewery become, samples were being sent to ports as far south as Charleston, South Carolina, and sold at auction at an advance of four dollars a barrel on the standard New York price. With brewing once again a growing industry, new brewhouses appeared in Albany and Rochester as well. In the former, James Boyd erected a massive brewery in 1796, with a capacity of about four thousand barrels a year. His son Robert would go on to form a partnership with Hawthorn McCulloch in 1808, and the alliance they forged would continue brewing beer for the next hundred years.

In Philadelphia, it was porter—a darker, maltier, English-style beer—that buoyed the industry. The quality improved drastically after the Revolution, as the general lack of British competition and restriction allowed the local industry to fully mature. A visiting Frenchman named Brissot de Warville would call Philadelphia beer "equal to the English: the manufacture of it saves a vast tribute formerly paid to the English industry." Another foreign commentator would note that "even English palates have been deceived by it. This discovery is a real service to America, for by it they are relieved of a tax to English industry." Led by brew families like the Hare, Haines, and Morris clans, the city was supplying, by the turn of the nineteenth century, beer to almost every major city in America, not to mention the Caribbean. And far from being contained to the seaboard, brewing went west as well. The rough-and-tumble fort city of Pittsburgh could boast its first major brewery by 1796, owned by the brewer Peter Shiras, who became prominent enough in local circles to leave a street named after him, if not an actual brewery.

The total number of breweries in New York and Philadelphia surged following the American Revolution, increasing steadily through 1810; that year, of the 132 major breweries in America, 48 were in Pennsylvania and 42 in New York alone. The secretary of the Treasury at that time, Albert Gallatin, would cite "malt liquors" as one of the new country's most firmly established industries, "supplying in several instances the greater, and in all a considerable part of the consumption of the United States."

Indeed, in the last decade of the eighteenth century, and the first of the nineteenth, it appeared American beer was on the fast track, thanks to an entrepreneurial brewing spirit that stretched back to the very first days of Dutch settlement in the Middle Colonies. America, it seemed, had once again become a country of beer drinkers.

That was, until the bottom fell out. The onset of America's postrevolutionary brewing renaissance had been encouraging, but the nation's beer revival was not to last. By the 1820s, what had been a promising and distinctly American industry was once again teetering on the brink. According to one source, the value of the brewing industry in Philadelphia in 1819 had dropped from $91,050 to $35,000 in less than five years. In an 1820 census, American breweries across the board were reporting "Sales diminished" and "Sales decreased." After a brief upswing on the heels of independence, the entire American beer industry suddenly awoke in the gutter again.

As for the reason behind the rapid decline, that same 1820 census report would go on to state it quite clearly: "Business diminished in consequence of the increased consumption of whiskey." The American Revolution might have ended the hegemony of British rum, but it left a void in the collective palate of a people who, although fond of beer as a table beverage, still liked to get drunk on hard liquor. And, as it would also turn out, independence opened up a huge swath of the frontier to western expansion, especially in the region that constituted western Virginia—what we know today as Kentucky and Tennessee. While the South had not had much success making a palatable beer of its own, the settlers in its mountainous hinterlands did know a thing or two about distilling even the shoddiest beer and turning it into barrel-aged whiskey. Rum might have been on its way out, but thanks to a new immigrant group taming the rough edges of the South, a new spirit would emerge to knock American beer off its perch . . . for a while, anyway.

And so it came to pass that in the year 1837—just two years before Abner Doubleday is alleged to have invented baseball in Cooperstown, New York, and less than a decade before the Knickerbocker Club of New York City would write the sport's first rulebook—the dilapidated ruins of the once-mighty Coulter Brewery, too far gone to be used for the making of beer, would be converted into one of New York City's first tenements, in the soon-to-be-legendary Five Points slum. American beer had swung and missed, but fortunately for beer lovers—even those content with an ice-cold Bud at a ball game—it had not quite struck out.

CHAPTER 3

❧

THE SOUTH

or

A Little Dixie Goes

a Long Way

THESE DAYS, YOU CAN FIND A GREAT MANY THINGS AT THE Old Absinthe House bar on Bourbon Street. There's the plethora of Louisiana football helmets, collecting dust and hanging from strings. There are the vintage signs advertising their signature old-time cocktails, like the absinthe frappe and the mint julep, testaments to the city's tangy blend of French and American pedigrees. There are the history lessons inherent in a place that's been around for two centuries and has seen everyone from Andrew Jackson and Robert E. Lee, to Mark Twain and Oscar Wilde get liquored up upon its stools. And yes, finally, there's even the absinthe, legal again after a hundred years, served beside the original marble absinthe fountain.

One thing you will not find, however, is Dixie beer—I know, I just asked. The bartender frowned and pointed instead to the small selection of mildly appealing micro- and macrobrews available on tap. It is a puzzling lacuna, given it's one of the South's few historic regional beers—a brewer by the name of Valentine Merz brought Dixie to the Crescent City way back in 1907. This part of the country has traditionally been more of an importer of beer than a producer, but Dixie is a notable exception. New Orleans's unique position at the very end of the Mississippi has always provided the southern port city with a steady influx of northern grain and European immigrants—two catalysts that always seem to give beer a boost. To visit the birthplace of one of the South's oldest and most storied local beers without sampling a bottle or two feels negligent at best. In fact, finally getting to try a Dixie was one of my primary reasons for hitting the French Quarter tonight—it's even mentioned in *A Confederacy of Dunces;* how could I not? When it comes to learning first-hand about the history of brewing in the region, Dixie is as close to a Holy Grail as you're going to get, which is why its absence is all the more galling. But as the saying goes, when life gives you lemons, have an absinthe instead. I forsake my "research" for a few moments and order one up, something so many writers and raconteurs did here so long ago. Yes, the establishment has taken on a bit of a sports-bar patina over the years, and indeed, you are more likely to see tourists from the Midwest than besotted southern writers. But if you squint your eyes and roll the wormwood-flavored spirit upon your tongue, you can almost imagine how the place must once have been . . . or if you're lucky, hallucinate it as such. For better or worse, no visions come, and the friendly tourists from St. Louis and the dangling football helmets maintain their real, albeit familiar charm.

My next stop is the famous Napoleon House, a place where, according to legend, the little Corsican himself was once offered refuge during exile. The beleaguered general never made it over, but the establishment does boast a fine collection of paintings and busts in tribute to the man, and to southern hospitality. Classical music wafts from the dining room, and a mustachioed bartender asks what I'd like. After a quick glance, I notice that both Dixie and Dixie Jazz are on the menu. But the bartender confirms my worst fears: the New Orleans beer is not available this night. So I take their legendary Sazerac cocktail instead, made from northern rye whiskey with a dash of bitters, and follow that up with—and I'm embarrassed to admit it, but such things happen—a hurricane. Essentially fruit

The Old Absinthe House has been getting the good people of New Orleans liquored up for more than two centuries. The abundance of Caribbean rum, northern rye whiskey, and French absinthe is a legacy of a southern plantation economy in which most manufactured goods had to be imported—alcohol included.

punch, mixed with a healthy portion of Caribbean rum, it's perhaps not the smartest choice for a writer pursuing research, but then again, New Orleans has never been known to foster good decision making.

At last taken by the spirt of New Orleans, and ready to let the *bon temps rouler,* I make my way to Frenchmen Street. Just off Esplanade, the strip is somewhat removed from the gaudy allures of Bourbon Street, but no less lively. Jazz and blues, the rich legacy of nearly four centuries of African American culture in the South, seeps from every entryway, and the streets are teeming with people drinking—yes, *drinking*—on the street, something you seldom see outside the Big Easy. The music sounds especially good coming from the bar d.b.a., and I poke my head inside, hoping they might actually have some Dixie on tap. And while the beer list here is a bit more promising, and includes such local delights as NOLA Blond, Abita Amber, and the decidedly Cajun-sounding Bayou Teche Miel Sauvage, alas, there is no Dixie. The beer that made New Orleans famous is apparently not so easy to find. The Abita, however, is quite pleasing on the palate, especially when served alongside a heaping helping of Delta Blues. I finish my first and treat myself to a second, which I pour into a to-go cup and proudly carry right back onto the street. What a town.

I've all but given up on finding my elusive Dixie, when I pass beneath the flashing neon sign of the Voodoo Mart liquor store. I hesitate, but decide it's worth a shot. I push my way through the dangling beads and desiccated alligator heads, toward the coolers way in the back. I peruse the beer offerings without much luck and consider calling it a night, when a green bottle catches my eye. There it is: Dixie beer. True, it's not terribly different from most of the other established pale lagers one finds in America, and there probably are a host of other more celebrated local beers to choose from. But none of them have the history of Dixie. A Louisiana staple for more than a hundred years, it's a rarity in a part of the country where locally based beers didn't really catch on until the craft brewing revival of the late twentieth century. And it's a survivor. Today Dixie isn't being made in Louisiana; it's contract brewed by a company in Wisconsin, although there is a growing movement to bring it back to New Orleans. Its reasons for relocating may be related directly to Hurricane Katrina—when the levees broke, it flooded the Dixie brewery—but it is telling from a historical perspective. While Dixie beer was actually made in the South for a full century, many of the other libations historically enjoyed south of the Mason-Dixon were not. As the French absinthes, northern rye Sazeracs, and Caribbean rum hurricanes I've enjoyed this night can attest, alcohol was, for much of the South's history, an imported product. Most manufactured goods, as a matter of fact, were imported products, in a society where plantation economics valued the exportation of a single crop above all else. It was a system kick-started way back in Jamestown, when Virginia's first settlers realized two things: barley didn't do too well in the southern heat, and tobacco did.

Nevertheless, there *was* brewing, with local styles defined primarily by innovative techniques specifically tailored for a warmer climate. The South can claim a brewing history all its own, beginning as early as the 1500s, when the first English explorers in the Tidewater discovered a strange new Indian grain could not only handle the warm southern climate—it could be malted and made into beer as well.

Corn.

Indeed, one could argue that American beer was born in the South, from the trial and error of those early English brewers who settled beside the Chesapeake. Their maize-based beverages never completely caught on, nor did commercial brewing in general (with the exception of a few well-positioned brands like Dixie, of course). But it wouldn't take long for a fresh batch of immigrants from backgrounds both Scottish and Irish to figure out perishable corn beer could be distilled quite easily into a corn whiskey that only improved with age. And there *certainly* was a market for that. The discovery would steer the course of American drinking habits for much of the nineteenth century, and bring the massive northern

In a region where local beer has historically been scarce, Dixie is a proud exception—although damage from Hurricane Katrina forced the label to leave the Crescent City.

beer industry to a standstill. This revelation had led me back to Bourbon Street this very night, for a shot of its namesake whiskey to finish the evening.

As soon as I finish this Dixie, that is.

To say the United States of America—and American beer, for that matter—has its origins in the South would be spot-on. Calling those first southern colonial ventures a success, however, would be stretching the truth. They were a disaster—at least at the beginning. And colonies and breweries were hobbled by many of the same problems: harsh climates, unfamiliar environs, and indigenous peoples not terribly inclined to bow before an unfamiliar king.

Men in Louisiana unload a truck filled with Jax beer, another one of the few southern labels. The beer was brewed in Jacksonville, Florida, from 1913 until 1956.

England's awkward entrée into New World colonialism began in the fifteenth century with John Cabot, a.k.a. Giovanni Caboto. Although Italian by birth, the mariner had made a home for himself in the seaports of Britain and was just as consumed as Christopher Columbus with finding a westward passage to the rich trading ports of Asia. Of course, Columbus found nothing of the kind, but rather an entirely new set of continents. Cabot was no doubt enraged when his *paisan* beat him to the punch in 1492, but he was also intrigued, and petitioned King Henry VII for permission to set out and claim at least some of those new lands, for England. King Henry encouraged would-be explorers to do the following:

Upon their own proper costs and charges to seek out, discover, and find whatsoever isles, countries, regions, or provinces of the heathen and infidels, whatsoever they be, and in what part of the world soever they be, which before this time have been unknown to Christians.

Politically correct, the fifteenth century was not, but ambitious, it was. Briefly, it looked as if England might catch up to its rival Spain in establishing a New World colony. In the summer of 1497, just five years after Columbus's first voyage, Cabot set out with a small crew from the port of Bristol and made the Atlantic crossing, with a ship almost certainly laden with ale and beer to nourish them on their voyage. In the weeks that followed, Cabot and his crew would nose their little caravel ship around the coast of what was most likely Newfoundland, taking note of the promising lands and fish-rich seas, but not bothering to advance on shore "beyond the shooting distance of a crossbow." Cabot returned to England after several weeks of scouting out the North American shore-line, to general fanfare and celebration—until an uprising in the Celtic lands of Cornwall distracted the king, delaying a second trip. When that second armada finally was put together to claim new lands for England the following year . . . well, nobody knows exactly what happened to it, although most historians assume it was lost at sea.

And so, while the sixteenth century saw Spain conquering the Caribbean and moving its attention to Mexico and South America, while Portugal was finding out just how big Brazil really was, and while the French were planting flags all across Quebec, England pretty much sat on its ass. Not that it didn't have plenty to occupy itself with back home; conflicts with the Catholic Church, political strife, and uprisings in its Celtic colonies kept the Crown busy. Keeping its own house in order was enough trouble—the idea of expanding the empire across a sea was a pipe dream at best.

At least, that is, until mind-boggling riches began pouring in from the colonies of its European rivals. Silver and gold came back by the shipload from Spanish territories in Central and South America; tobacco and sugar flooded the European market from the Caribbean isles. By the late sixteenth century, England was finally catching on to the fiscal necessity of New World settlement. It wasn't just about expanding boundaries—it was crucial to keeping up with its national competitors. Suddenly, England wanted in on the game. The Crown's first colonies would be in Virginia, yet from the beginning, they would be financial ventures, aimed at duplicating the influx of riches that its European contenders had been enjoying for almost a century.

The English inspiration for New World colonization may have come from Spain, but their model of colonization was much closer to home. Just as Spain had honed its somewhat harsh colonial skills during the Reconquista and in the subjugation of the Canary Islands prior to turning its attention to the Aztecs or the Incas, the English had learned a thing or two about claiming lands and displacing native peoples in its own conquest of Ireland. In terms of strategy and logistics, their initial attempt at colonizing the New World would capitalize on the lessons of that earlier invasion, alloting "plantations" in the Tidewater as they previously had in Ireland. The first batch of Virginia planters was drawn from very much the same class of landed aristocrats who were granted estates in Ireland, after the Flight of the Earls drained the Emerald Isle of its Gaelic aristocracy. The same colonial policies that England had refined in its subjugation of Ireland would be adapted and applied to coastal Virginia.

Assuming, of course, they could get a settlement and a

brewery going, both of which were crucial for a sustained English presence, and both of which proved exceedingly difficult. When the dashing Sir Walter Raleigh, himself a hero of the wars in Ireland, received permission from the "Virgin Queen" Elizabeth to found a colony in 1584, his initial attempt on Roanoke Island, as any student of American history can tell you, evidently ended in disaster. But it did have one important consequence: it was there that Englishmen brewed what was perhaps the first true European-American beer. Barley, as the English quickly noted, did not fare well in the southern heat—it was a cold-weather crop. Corn, on the other hand, an Indian grain entirely new to them, positively flourished. In a 1587 report aimed at encouraging immigration, an English settler of the Roanoke colony named Thomas Harriot would observe:

> The graine is about the bigness of our ordinary English peaze, and not much different in forme and shape: but of divers colours; some white, some red, some yellow, and some blew. All of them yield a very white and sweet flower: being used according to his kinde, it maketh a very good bread. We made of the same in the countrey some Mault, whereof was brewed as good Ale as was to be desired. So likewise by the helpe of Hops, therof may be made as good Beere.

Corn bread and corn beer would have been familiar to many Native American civilizations, but to those first English arrivals in the American South, they were totally novel—and, as they discovered, quite tasty. But that revelation met a serious hurdle. The colony vanished, for reasons historians still can't agree upon, and southern beer would have to be patient.

The wait wasn't long, though. Under the auspices of the Virginia Company of London, and with a little help from John Rolfe (not to mention Pocahontas), another colony was established in Jamestown in 1607, and it fared somewhat better. In the years that followed, well-to-do country gentlemen from across southern and western England were given plantations to mind, and lower-class inhabitants of London and its environs were invited to do most of the heavy lifting as indentured servants. And just as in Roanoke, colonists were eager to find a sustainable drink, with "wine being too dear, and barely changeable and hard to grow." Importing wine from Europe was astronomically expensive, and English barley withered in the southern sun. Again, corn came to the rescue. George Thorpe, an early overseer at the Berkeley Hundred plantation, was desperately searching for a solution to Virginia's early liquor woes when he stumbled upon the same solution Thomas Harriot had almost four decades before, writing to a friend back in England:

> Wee have found a waie to make soe good drink of Indian corne I hae divers times refused to drinke good stronge English beare and chose to drink that.

But alas, the curse of southern beer would strike again. For it seemed seeking out sources of alcohol wasn't George Thorpe's only hobby—he had been charged with founding what amounted to one of the first Indian schools, aimed at assimilating the native Powhatan people and absorbing their lands. Needless to say, the Indians were less enthusiastic about the idea than the English settlers, and in 1622, George Thorpe was killed in an uprising of the Powhatans, a people who were amenable to sharing their grains with the new colonists, but far less willing to forfeit their sacred way of life.

There was another plant besides corn that fared well in Virginia: tobacco. John Rolfe had smuggled a few seeds of the sweeter Caribbean variety up from Trinidad, and with that first crop of *Nicotiana tabacum* planted in 1611, the course of the South was officially set. With the old "plantation" system of agrarian allotment already in place in the new colony, it wasn't a terribly great stretch to adapt it slightly to the production of tobacco. The chance at a gentlemanly fortune attracted the adventurous sons of aristocratic families from across the southern English countryside to try their luck as Virginia planters. Some were unable to inherit lands back home for reasons of primogeniture; others were from families who had fought on the wrong side of the English Civil War. All saw a plantation in the New World as a way to get rich.

What began with tobacco in Virginia would spread to other southern colonies as well and come to include sugar, rice, indigo, and eventually the biggest plantation crop of them all, cotton. With the local agrarian economies fully dedicated to the harvesting and exporting of a single and highly profitable crop, there was little impetus to invest money or resources in the manufacture of goods on a large, industrial scale. Beer, while still beloved by southerners, was no exception. Commercial brewing was exceedingly difficult in the early South; neither barley nor hops fared well in the heat, and in an age before refrigeration or commercial shipping, any beer produced would not last long enough for distribution, given the region's long summers, lack of roads, and widely dispersed plantation settlements. It's not that the early inhabitants of the southern colonies didn't want beer—they simply lacked the barley, the hops, and the infrastructure to make it a viable commercial product.

The one group of southerners who did possess the experience and expertise to brew a truly local beer in the southern

With the discovery that tobacco could be grown on plantations in colonial Virginia, the South's economic course was set for the next two centuries. Here, barrels are loaded with tobacco leaves to be shipped to foreign ports. Money gained from the sale of plantation crops could be used to buy imported products, beer and other libations among them.

climate were also the one group generally forbidden to do so. As early as 1619, Jamestown was already using forced African labor; by the middle of the seventeenth century, slavery had become institutionalized and legally recognized in Virginia, replacing indentured servitude as the primary source of plantation labor, and spreading beyond to the colonies of

Maryland and Carolina. It would exist in New England and New York as well, but the plantation system that encouraged the slave trade never took root there, and while the institution declined in the North, it became a mainstay of the emerging southern economy. During the colonial period, some six hundred thousand enslaved Africans would endure the horrors of the Middle Passage and be taken against their will to America.

The first African Americans brought few if any material possessions, but culturally, they came to America with their own distinct traditions in language, religion, music, food,* and yes, brewing. Africans from a wide range of ethnicities and cultural backgrounds had been brewing and fermenting alcoholic drinks with ingredients other than barley for thousands of years. Both biblical and archaeological evidence supports the existence of brewed beverages made from emmer wheat in Egypt and Ethiopia. A Portuguese explorer from the sixteenth century noted the abundance of fermented honey mead in West Africa; in the Congo and in Angola, a palm wine was preferred, and across sub-Saharan Africa, beers brewed from sorghum,† millet, and even plantains were enjoyed, as they still are to this day. *Pombe, tembo dolo, burukutu, tchakpalo*—all are produced in warmer climates where European barley simply does not thrive, and all have roots that stretch back well before the arrival of European-style brewing.

One can imagine how the South might have developed a host of local, African-inspired sorghum beers and palm wines

---

*Two of the defining characteristics of southern cuisine—frying and the use of hot and tangy sauces—both have their origins in the culinary traditions of West Africa. And as for gumbo, the name itself is believed to come from the Bantu word for okra, *ki ngombo.*

†Interesting side note: A version of Guinness Foreign Extra Stout is brewed in Nigeria that uses local sorghum as opposed to imported barley. No other Guinness FES has ever attempted or been allowed to do this.

to call its own, as an alternative to the barley-based concoctions preferred in the cooler North. After all, it had been African slaves in the Caribbean who had first discovered and shown Europeans how sugar cane molasses could be distilled into spirituous rum. It's quite likely that under more permissive circumstances, various forms of African beer could have been adopted in the American South as well. In addition to the many basic freedoms they were deprived of, though, slaves were also generally forbidden to make or consume alcohol. Masters usually frowned on the practice, and many states actually banned it.

With fines and possible prison time on the line, slaves were rarely involved with alcohol consumption or production. There are some exceptions, though. George Washington was known to employ slaves in distilling and probably brewing as well at his Mount Vernon plantation in the late 1700s. Documents indicate the Baumgardner Distillery of Augusta County, Virginia, owned and hired slave brewers and distillers just a few decades later. And across the South, Christmas was an occasion when many plantations permitted drinking *and* brewing among the slave population. Subsequently, enslaved Americans of African descent created their own resourceful methods for providing a festive holiday beverage when commercially produced alcohol was not provided for them—which, on special occasions, it sometimes was. Persimmons grew wild in the forests that bordered many farms and plantations, and when occasion allowed, they were used as a brewing ingredient.* West Turner, a former slave from Louisiana, recalls such resourcefulness:

---

*African Americans may have been among the first to brew a persimmon beer with sweet potatoes and corn as adjuncts, although there is evidence that the Cherokee made a persimmon wine. As records exist of early southerners of both English and African descent including persimmons in alcoholic drinks, it seems likely that they learned about the ingredient early on from their Native American neighbors.

The continent of Africa has rich brewing traditions all its own, often incorporating grains other than barley. In this illustration, *pombe* is being brewed using ground millet. In the American South, however, enslaved Africans were generally prohibited from brewing—although there were rare occasions when their unique skills could be put into practice.

> We made persimmon beer, too. Just stuck our persimmons in a keg with two or three gallons of water and sweet potato peelings and some hunks of corn bread and left it there until it began to work.

Similar recipes come from Mississippi, Georgia, Maryland, and Arkansas, giving some evidence that the practice of making homemade persimmon beer was relatively widespread throughout the South, and generally involved a similar recipe of corn, sweet potato peelings, and persimmons. The seeds of the locust plant could also be brewed into a beer, and according to many accounts, the beverage was nearly as popular as persimmon beer for special occasions. Charlie Hudson, who had once been a slave in Georgia, would recall:

Christmas we went from house to house looking for locust and persimmon beer. Children went to all the houses hunting gingerbread. Ma used to roll it thin, cut it out with a thimble, and give a dozen of them little balls to each child. Persimmon beer and gingerbread! What big times we did have at Christmas.

So, although heavily restricted, small-scale brewing did occur in antebellum African American communities. Relying on local southern ingredients and African traditions of non-barley-based brewing that stretched back hundreds if not thousands of years, they were able to provide, even under exceptionally difficult circumstances, their own unique regional beer to help celebrate the holidays.

The more privileged segments of southern society, meanwhile, failed to achieve quite the same success of their northern counterparts in brewing. Nevertheless, they did have options when it came to drinking. Some simply found alternatives to local beer. Those with enough money enjoyed imported Madeira wine, a fortified alcoholic product that could not only survive the warm summers—it actually improved under warm conditions. A prominent feature of colonial plantation homes was the presence of a Madeira loft in the attic, a place where the casks could ripen in the rising heat. Virginia dram, a brandy made from the peaches introduced to the region in the seventeenth century, was also a popular drink of the colonial era in the South. And of course there was rum, enjoyed in Virginia, the Carolinas, Maryland, and Georgia, just as it was in the English colonies to the north. Either shipped in directly from the Caribbean, or from the rum-producing distilleries of New England, it proved to be the common southern spirit of the colonial era as well.

Imported Madeira and rum may have filled the gap when

it came to wetting southern whistles in the seventeenth and eighteenth centuries, but one mustn't forget that the plantation culture of the lowland South was fundamentally English in origin, with many of the most prominent families hailing from either rural aristocratic estates or wealthy clans of London merchants. And while their plantation society was formed under a fundamentally different economic and cultural model than the staunchly middle-class Puritans in New England, they shared more with their northern cousins than an inability to pronounce R's. The English predilection for beer very much persisted—the conundrum was how best to get it.

Unlike New England and New Netherland, where drinking often centered around the trade guilds and taverns that dominated town and city life, much of the drinking and entertaining in the plantation South was conducted in the home—farms were widely dispersed, and urban centers few and far between. For that reason, the home brewing of low-alcohol "small" beer became a common practice, just as it had been in rural English estates for centuries. The following recipe penned by George Washington, both founding father and true Virginia aristocrat, gives some idea of what a typical home brew on a southern plantation would have consisted of in the late seventeenth and early eighteenth centuries:

> Take a large Sifter of Bran Hops to your Taste—Boil these 3 hours. Then strain out 30 Gallons into a Cooler, put in 3 Gallons Molasses while the Beer is scalding hot or rather drain the molasses into the Cooler & strain the Beer on it while boiling Hot. Let this stand till it is little more than Blood warm. Then put in a quart of Yeast if the weather is very cold, cover it over with a Blanket & let it work in the Cooler 24 Hours. Then put it into

the Cask—leave the Bung open till it is almost done Working—Bottle it that day Week it was brewed.

Worth noting here is the primary ingredient: molasses. With limited barley malt to add into the mix, southerners found other fermentable sugars with which to brew, allowing the rural English practice of domestic brewing to persist in the colonial American South, albeit with slightly altered ingredients.[*] Evidently, such impromptu southern beers, be they made with molasses, as the gentry seemed to prefer, or persimmons, which slaves and others without access to processed sugars used when they were able, could actually turn out quite good—even by finicky British standards. A molasses small beer was surely a rich and sweet accompaniment to a colonial meal, perhaps even akin to a weak stout, and a persimmon beer made from wild yeast, one can only imagine, was almost certainly a tart and refreshing treat—the fruity southern lambic of its day. An Englishman passing through Maryland in the early 1700s made the following observation of the local beer:

> The beer they brew is excellent, which they make in great Quantities, of Parsimons, &c., of Molasses; for few of them are Come to malting their corn, of any kind, at which I was much surprised; as even the Indian Grain, as I have found experimentally, will produce an wholesome and generous Liquor.

---

[*]As to the origins of beer made from molasses, it's difficult to pinpoint them exactly. Records of alcoholic drinks made from sugar cane go back all the way to ancient India and China, and early American colonists in both the North and South did use molasses to varying degrees for brewing. It's not implausible, however, that the practice became widespread thanks to the ingenuity of Africans in the New World. As molasses beer is essentially the precursor to rum, it seems likely that the practice became popular first among slaves in the Caribbean, before being picked up and brought to the kitchens of the American colonies. If this was the case, then one could argue that African brewing traditions did indirectly help create a form of beer that was widespread in the South.

As this traveler astutely notes, local grain supplies were not generally malted or used in brewing—whatever grain was cultivated would have been used for cooking in the Big House, or given out to feed field hands and livestock. In most cases, improvised small beers made from available ingredients formed the closest thing to a true locally made southern brew, and even those types of beverages were seldom brewed on a commercial scale, but rather made in the kitchens of southern plantations, to be consumed domestically by the family and its guests, and on special occasions, by the slaves who toiled long hours in the neighboring fields.

But does that mean no good, strong beer was available in the early colonial South? Hardly. For just as the exportation of plantation crops brought tobacco to England, so did the establishment of transatlantic trade routes bring English beer to the southern colonies, through most of the seventeenth and eighteenth centuries. Thanks to that imported beer, early southerners were able to keep alive the drinking traditions of the homeland.

With the addition of new southern colonies, the market for malty imports only grew. When Georgia was established in 1733, its landed elite drew from the same class as Virginia and the Carolinas to the north. Under the leadership of a south English aristocrat named James Edward Oglethorpe, whose family hailed from the ancestral estate in the Surrey town of Godalming, the colony received its official charter. One marked difference, though—Oglethorpe initially banned slavery in the infant colony, and along with it, large planta-tion estates. Something of an idealist, Oglethorpe envisioned a settlement where men of all classes and creeds owned and worked their own land. Oglethorpe was also an early tem-perance advocate and prohibited strong spirits in the colony. Again, English beer wasn't the only import—rum, from both the Caribbean and the distilleries of New England, was beginning to flood the southern market. In typical English fashion, however, Oglethorpe saw beer not as an intoxicant, but a necessity for daily life. Oglethorpe even went so far as to distribute beer rations to thirsty colonists, first issued upon their arrival and continued so long as they remained residents of Georgia. Eventually, the alcohol options for early Georgians reflected what was available through much of the southern colonies, rum excepted: "Strong-beer from England, Melasses for brewing [small] Beer, and Madeira Wines, which the People might purchase at reasonable Rates."

Given the dearth of other options, early Georgians did attempt to brew some "strong" beer of their own, to augment local molasses small beers and imported English beer. Major William Horton, who oversaw Jekyll Island in the 1740s, was among the very first English settlers in Georgia to try brewing on a larger scale. In 1746, a visitor to his farm took note of "a very Large Barnfull of Barley not inferior to ye Barley in England," among other seemingly flourishing crops. Just one year later, Horton ordered a "Great Copper" pot, ostensibly to begin turning some of that barley into drinkable beer. But his dream of a commercial Georgian brewery was not to be. Whatever barley that visitor took note of appeared to be either a fluke, or surreptitiously imported—by 1748, he would admit defeat, writing that his holdings on Jekyll Island were "totally unfit for cultivation," and his brewery was scrapped. Ultimately, Major Horton ran into the same problem as his southern brewing predecessors: the barley he needed to make English-style beer simply did not thrive in the local climate, and the basic economics of plantation agriculture didn't lend themselves to the development of local industry. Sadly, within a year, William Horton succumbed to what was very likely malaria, "to the universal sorrow of all his acquaintances." Alas, yet again, a noble attempt at a commercial southern beer ended in an unfortunate disaster. Had things turned out different, perhaps Georgians, even coastal southerners as a whole, would be sipping on cold bottles of Horton's Jekyll Island Ale to this very day—but that was not the case. By 1751, a group of immigrants from Salzburg, attracted initially to Georgia by its reputation as a land of freedom and opportunity, were disappointed to learn the following:

> At this time . . . [A] brewer is not needed for as yet too little barley is grown; and the inhabitants who have the ability to cook a healthy beer for themselves out of syrup [molasses], Indian corn and hops, or the tops of the white and water firs, which is very cheap. Strong barley beer comes from New York, at times also from England. A quart of which is worth 4d. It is cheaper by the barrel. In these lands little beer is drunk.

James Oglethorpe's vision was not to be—upon losing its charter, Georgia became another royal colony, and as such, another part of an increasingly thirsty and import-dependent South. But as the passage above clearly indicates, southern drinking habits were changing by the mid-eighteenth century. For starters: with the idea of a unique "American" identity congealing, and the revolution that would win it its own nation just a few decades away, southerners were finally catching on to the use of native "Indian corn" as an ingredient in their local beers, as opposed to simply using Caribbean molasses. And more important, although the strong beer consumed was still being imported at that time, the bulk of it was no longer coming from England, but from New York. Both New York and Philadelphia possessed an entrepreneurial climate favorable to large-scale industry, and a burgeoning commercial beer industry to boot. In a development that no doubt irked British breweries to no end, the two cities by the mid-eighteenth century had a brewing industry that could compete directly with British imports. According to the *Virginia Gazette,* which reported quite regularly on imports of Philadelphia beer to the southern colony, between April of 1765 and April of 1766, a total of 1,288 barrels of Philly's passed through its ports. And while individual shipments of only six or seven barrels were commonplace in the 1740s and 1750s, by 1774, with the American colonies on the very cusp of open rebellion, single shipments of thirty barrels were not uncommon. America's allegiance to a foreign king was wavering, but its thirst was not; by the 1760s and 1770s, many Americans began to voice the idea that they deserved their own country, and more than a few Americans had given up English beer in favor of something a little more domestic.

Included among them was the original founding father himself, George Washington. Like many southern aristocrats, George had a predilection for foreign Madeira wine and imported porters. When tensions finally escalated into all-out war with the British, though, the patriotic southern officer ceased ordering his porter from England and became the enthusiastic customer of a Philadelphia brewer named Robert Hare—a practice he would continue well after the war was won. Following an especially festive Fourth of July parade in the city in 1788, Washington would write the following to a local friend, with a mischievous wink: "I beg you will send me a gross of Mr. Hairs best bottled Porter if the price is not much enhanced by the copious droughts you took of it at the late Procession." Evidently, he had second thoughts and actually decided to order *more* of Mr. Hare's fine Philly porter. Just two weeks later, he would follow up that request with the following:

As the price of Porter according to your Account has not been enhanced and is good in quality, I beg if this letter gets to hand in time, that you would add another gross to the one ordered in my former letter.

If there were any lingering doubts among foreigners as to the prospects of America or its beer, Washington dispelled them quite peremptorily one year later in the following missive to his good war buddy, the Marquis de Lafayette:

We have already been too long subject to British prejudices. I use no porter or cheese in my family, but such as is made in America: both these articles may now be purchased of an exceptional quality.

Like his revolutionary brother Benjamin Franklin, Washington espoused the idea of severing the bonds of foreign dependency when it came to alcohol and replacing it instead with a tall glass of self-reliance, by drinking beer that was American, if not southern. Even a man as tenacious as Washington ran into the same hurdles as the many would-be southern brewers before him. In the year 1787, while George was no doubt savoring Philly porter, his own barley crop at Mount Vernon was a total failure. He would write to Colonel Clement Biddle that "my Barley, this year, shared the same fate with my other crops. The drought during the summer was so excessive that I cannot form any just opinion of what it might produce in a seasonable year." Whether it was sixteenth-century Roanoke, seventeenth-century Jamestown, or eighteenth-century Mount Vernon, it did not matter: the thirst for beer was there, but the barley to brew it simply was not.

Southerners tried anyway. The "Home brew'd is best" slogan that brewers rallied around in New York and Philadelphia was eagerly adopted by some southerners as well, who, with English imports dwindling, were willing to try their hand at brewing. The advertisements posted in Virginia publications of that period certainly indicate a market for those with skills in brewing, as well as the equipment with which to do it. According to the *Virginia Gazette,* a man named John Mercer was offering to fill bottles sent to his brewery in Marlborough "with beer and porter at 6s. or with ale at 4s." The partners Joseph Jones and William Woodford collaborated on a sizable brewery in Fredericksburg in 1771, consisting of a "Brewhouse, Malthouse, Counting-House, Cooper's Shop, &c. all new, and in good Order for carrying on the Brewing Business." Unfortunately, simply having the proper equipment to brew was not the same thing as running a successful brewery. Just three years later, their failed Fredericksburg brewery was for sale, and although the exact outcome of John Mercer's brewery is not recorded, it seems to have met a similar fate. Making commercially viable beer in the South was difficult at best; competing with the huge breweries of Philadelphia and New York was all but impossible.

Competing when it came to beer, anyway. The eighteenth century saw at first a trickle, and then a deluge of immigrants hailing from lands where beer was not simply brewed—it was distilled. And while southern beer would never hold a candle to its northern competition, southern *whiskey* as sketched out above, would drive the American beer industry to the brink of extinction for a sizable part of the nineteenth century. All thanks to a feisty people we've come to know as the Scots-Irish.

The notion of "drink" in Scotland and Ireland is practically synonymous with whiskey. In fact, the word *whiskey* itself derives from *uisce beatha,* Gaelic for "water of life," and the origins of whiskey lie in the medieval histories of those two Celtic nations. Long before they were sipping on single malts or pounding the poteen, though, the Celtic and pre-Celtic peoples of both lands were enthusiastic drinkers of beer. In fact, some of the earliest archaeological evidence for beer consumption in Europe comes from northern Scotland. On an excavation of stone circles in the Isle of Arran, pottery with traces of grain and honey were found and dated to 3000 B.C. At Kinloch, on the Isle of Rhum, Neolithic pot shards dated to 2000 B.C. indicated traces of mashed cereal straw, cereal pollens, and meadowsweet—a common ancient beer flavoring. Should any classical scholarship be needed to verify the assumption that these ancient peoples were drinking beer, it comes by way of the Greek explorer Pytheas of Massalia, who wrote of a misty land in the north of the British Isles, close to the "frigid zone," whose inhabitants relied heavily on a drink made from honey and grain—the occasional tipple to ward off the chill was apparently as much appreciated by Scotland's early inhabitants as it is today.

Just across the Celtic Sea, beer shared a similar popularity. The enjoyment of brewed drinks in Ireland predates Christianity by centuries, likely even millennia. Pagan Irish mythology makes frequent reference to the drink. The fabled Ulster Cycle is filled with references to beer and mead halls, much like the Germanic mythology of England and Scandinavia, and in the Finn Cycle, the warrior Fothad refused to drink his beer without the severed heads of his enemies to garnish it. Severed heads aside, things seemed to have changed little with the coming of Christianity via Saint Patrick in the fifth century. St. Brigit was certainly the most celebrated brewer of Irish beer in the early Christian period, and when her own brewery came up short, she relied on divine intervention: a number of her reported miracles involved turning water into beer, be it for midwives, lepers, or at least in one case, an entire diocese of eighteen churches.

In fact, the Celtic enthusiasm for Christianity and beer would effectively introduce monastic brewing to Europe, as Hiberno-Scottish monks took their missions to the Continent. But cultural exchange is a two-way street. While Celtic missionaries helped encourage brewing in European monasteries farther south during the medieval period, the friars of Spain and Italy were learning a few tricks of their own—including the old Arab technique of liquid distillation, which proved handy for turning wine into something far more potent and durable. And they were not shy about sharing this fact with their religious brethren to the north.

One small problem: For while grapes abounded in Spain and Italy, they didn't exactly thrive in Scotland and Ireland. Grain, on the other hand, did. While the Latinate monks of southern Europe got pretty good at turning wine into brandy, Celtic distillers discovered the same technique could work just as well with beer. Simply by heating their barley brew in a copper pot still, collecting the alcohol vapors, and cooling them back into a liquid, they learned to duplicate the process, albeit with a different alcoholic beverage in mind. This "distilled beer," as whiskey truly was, would never completely eclipse actual beer in Scotland and Ireland, but it would certainly give it a run for its money. With the rise of the Scots-Irish distillers of the early nineteenth century, the same pattern would eventually emerge in America as well.

The predecessors of the Scots-Irish were relatively poor farmers from the southern Lowlands of Scotland. As English-speaking Protestants—albeit Presbyterians—they were recruited by the English to populate the "plantations" in the Irish province of Ulster and were relied upon as a natural buffer against the Gaelic-speaking Catholics they had displaced. Beginning in 1609 with the Plantation of Ulster, large numbers of these Scottish border people began arriving in Ireland, where they were granted tracts of tenant land on farms confiscated from the native population. Over the century that followed, the "Ulster Scots" would become entrenched in the north of Ireland, as assistants in a British policy of cultural assimilation, and as the first line of defense in the many bloody rebellions and uprisings that ensued because of it.

Obviously, this wasn't the most secure position to be in, and many sought better opportunities across the sea. Between 1717 and 1775, perhaps as many as a quarter million Ulster Scots emigrated to America, lured by the promise of unclaimed land and religious freedom. The coastal areas of Virginia, Maryland, and the Carolinas were dominated by large commercial plantations, but the rugged frontier to the west was up for the taking—especially following the American Revolution. The British had discouraged settlement beyond the Appalachians, concerned about potential French and Native American hostility on the other side. Once their independence was won, however, Americans were all for it, and the land-craving, freedom-loving, whiskey-making Scots-Irish were happy to be at the vanguard, and more than willing to trade in their skills with a musket for a chance at finally owning their own farm.

East of the Appalachian Mountains, early whiskey-making settlers had relied heavily on rye for distilling. It was relatively common, easy to grow, and cheap to buy. After Daniel Boone led the first batch of settlers through the Cumberland Gap, all that changed. As pioneers filtered down into what was to become Kentucky, Tennessee, and West Virginia, they quickly came around to what southern settlers as far back as Roanoke had already discovered: the native corn fared far better in the summer heat than any other grain. But unlike their somewhat snobby English predecessors, who had been reluctant to use rugged Indian corn as a substitute for fine British barley, the Scots-Irish had no qualms making whiskey out of it—adaptation is, after all, the key to frontier survival.

This changed everything. With the arrival of a whole new drink to the tavern scene, the brief beer revival that followed the American Revolution came to a screeching halt. Yes, rum was out of the picture, but frontier whiskey wasn't far behind it. Americans had learned to do precisely what Benjamin Franklin had hoped—create a spirit from our own native grains. But in doing so, the sudden abundance of inexpensive whiskey struck a tremendous blow to our native beer industry. In an age of frontier expansion, whiskey just made far more sense. Beer was a perishable commodity that, even with the most hops and best of intentions, couldn't be transported commercially across bumpy frontier roads during hot southern summers. Whiskey, on the other hand, not only survived the journey—it actually improved in quality as it aged and experienced temperature change. By the early nineteenth century, even cities on the East Coast were being flooded by this new "western" whiskey, and discovering to their surprise that after months of travel, it was actually quite good. This passage from an 1818 distilling manual states what was happening in fairly unambiguous terms:

> The rapidity of improvements in the western parts of the United States, is a matter of some consideration to the distillers of the Atlantic States. They have already made considerable progress in the art of distillation, and the vast quantities of grain which are produced by their fertile lands, beyond the necessary consumption, cannot be so well disposed of in any way as in pork and whiskey. Here we already find Tennessee and Kentucky whiskey in our sea ports, and it is generally preferred to that made

nearer home; this by the way, is a powerful argument against the common prejudice against using corn, and the western whiskey is chiefly made of that grain . . . As they depend upon the rise of the rivers to send their whiskey to market, it acquires some age: this also, and the motion of travelling, has considerable effect on improving it.

Even George Washington, the great porter lover and beer advocate of the South, would get in on the whiskey game, founding one of the country's first large commercial whiskey distilleries at Mount Vernon in 1797. He used both rye and corn in his recipe and experienced great success in selling it to his friends and neighbors. In short order, what had been a fringe drink of Indian traders and Scots-Irish mountaineers was suddenly being enjoyed by Virginia planters with aristocratic English pedigrees. And from there, its popularity would only continue to grow. In 1801, some 50,000 gallons of whiskey traveled through the Louisville Custom House in Kentucky on its way to market. In 1810, that number had increased to 250,000 gallons, and by 1822, it had reached 2,250,000 gallons, destined for bars, taverns, and general stores across the country. A new frontier west of the Appalachian Mountains was open, corn was being grown there in copious amounts thanks to the richness of the soil, and Scots-Irish settlers weren't just making beer out of it—they were distilling it and sending it down the river to be sold all over America. Beer on its own was bulkier by volume and could never survive the journey; whiskey was far more potent, and it most definitely didn't spoil with age.

The effect on the beer industry was of course disastrous. Whatever gains it had made with rum's demise in the wake of the Revolution were quickly nullified by whiskey's ascendancy. While the annual per capita consumption of commercially produced distilled spirits had rocketed to nearly five

Ultimately, it would be Scots-Irish pioneers on the rugged frontier who would solve the South's liquor woes. The warm climate and wild terrain may have been hostile to perishable corn beer, but corn *whiskey* only improved with age. In the late 1700s, bourbon was born, and it would eventually give the American beer industry a run for its money.

gallons in 1810—almost three times the present rate—annual per capita intake of commercial beer was under a gallon—some twenty times *less* than Americans drink today. In the young city of Cincinnati, the same 18 cents that could buy only a single bottle of beer in the early 1800s could purchase a half gallon of whiskey. Is it any wonder that Americans were increasingly choosing the latter? Even the brewery-heavy states of Pennsylvania and New York would end up reeling. In 1819, one estimate stated that the value of the entire beer industry had plummeted by nearly 60 percent in just four years. Matthew Vassar, one of the nation's few successful brewers of the era, would also lament what had become of America and its brewing industry from his office on the Hudson. "The times are awful, awful!," he exclaimed in a journal entry dated 1837, "worse than this or any other country witnessed." Thanks to the Scots-Irish settlers who populated the South's westernmost hinterlands, the region finally had its own commercially viable drink—but all that bourbon took a serious toll on even the most prominent American breweries.

Beer may have been in serious decline, but it still had its champions, even in the whiskey-drinking South. Foremost among them was a Virginia aristocrat named Thomas Jefferson. A great lover of drink, Jefferson had become a connoisseur of both wines and porters during his time in Paris and Philadelphia, respectively. And while he wasn't totally against stronger spirits when enjoyed in moderation, he was known to frequently lament "the poison of whiskey, which is destroying [the middle classes] by wholesale." He had labored together with James Madison to curb the new nation's craving for spirits in the aftermath of the Revolution, and he was a strong advocate of both wine and beer as local substitutes. Upon retiring to his Monticello estate at the end of his presidency in 1810, he took up the life of a country gentleman and devoted a great deal of time to the brewing of beer. In 1813, he feverishly hunted down a New York brewing manual called *The American Brewer & Maltster,* which included methods of malting Indian corn—a useful technique for a home brewer who lived in a region where barley did not fare well. He eventually corresponded with the author, Joseph Coppinger, an ambitious entrepreneur who approached the retired president with an intriguing proposition: a national brewery. Coppinger was a champion of "the establishment of a Brewing company at Washington as a National object," an endeavor that would "unquestionably tend to improve the quality of our Malt Liquors in every point of the Union and serve to counteract the baneful influences of ardent spirits on the health and Morals

The original American beer geek and home brewer himself, Thomas Jefferson. His dream of seeing the United States become a beer-drinking nation again would be realized, but not in his lifetime.

of our fellow Citizens. . . ." His asking price to establish the first "national" brewery in Washington? A mere $20,000.

It is possible that Coppinger was full of hot air, but it may also have been a brilliant idea. A federally sponsored brewery based in the nation's capital could have revived a flagging industry and allowed beer to replace whiskey in the urban centers of the coast. But alas, the nation would never find out. Jefferson liked the idea, but ultimately said no. While he admitted to sharing Coppinger's views on the dangers of spirits, and to brewing a great deal of beer for personal use with corn and wheat—his farm did not grow barley—he politely declined, writing that he was "too old & too fond of quiet to engage in new & distant undertakings." While perhaps a younger Thomas Jefferson would have embraced such a fiery idea, the retired Thomas Jefferson simply wanted to enjoy his dotage and the occasional fine glass of beer. He would continue to brew beer and experiment with various brewing techniques right up until his death in 1826—on the Fourth of July, interestingly enough.

Jefferson's legacy may not include the salvation of the American beer industry, but his résumé does contain the Louisiana Purchase of 1803, an unprecedented act of land acquisition that brought huge tracts of western territory, formerly French, directly into American possession. This included fresh access to the Mississippi River, as well as that lively jewel of a city at its terminus: New Orleans. With its thriving port and constant stream of river traffic, the town was unique in the American South, and its abundance of job opportunities attracted immigrants galore throughout the nineteenth century, one of whom happened to be a German man by the name of Georg Merz. As an aficionado of fine beer, Herr Merz was dismayed by the locally made southern-style beverages that greeted him upon his arrival in Louisiana—peculiar brews of "molasses and wormwood" that bore little resemblance to the crisp lagers he had known back home. He began brewing his own beer in 1855, at the Old Canal Steam Brewery on the Carondelet

Canal; thirteen years later, he would invite his nephew, Valentine Merz, to come work for him. Unlike his uncle Georg, young Valentine did not hail from old Deutschland—he was a first-generation German American, fresh off the farm in Indiana. Once settled in New Orleans, the eager and ambitious Valentine would go on to master the trade and, eventually, succeed in doing the one thing everyone from George Thorpe to Thomas Jefferson had failed to do: create a commercially viable southern beer. More specifically, he created Dixie beer, a brew beloved by New Orleanians and thirsty writers to this very day. But while Valentine Merz may have left behind the Middle West to seek his fortune, many more German Americans did not. And the breweries they founded in the nation's heartland would ultimately change beer—and America—forever.

Of course this means I'm going to have to drink as many of these Dixie beers as I can before I have to make my way back up north. Challenging research, to say the least—especially in a city like New Orleans, where so many seductive beverage options fill the menu, and southern hospitality is always on tap.

CHAPTER 4

THE MIDWEST

or

The German Beer Barons

Finally Hop to It

FOR A FAITHFUL BEER PILGRIM, THE MIDWEST HAS NO shortage of brewing meccas. There's St. Louis, with its massive Anheuser-Busch facility, one of the biggest in the world. Milwaukee boasts the historical architecture of Miller and Pabst, not to mention some darn good bratwurst. Chicago, too, is right there at the head of the pack when it comes to craft brewing in America's heartland, with local labels like the Goose Island Beer Company adding a host of unique brews to the regional repertoire. Cleveland may not be quite as renowned for its brewing history, but it does have one thing these illustrious beer capitals do not: Fred Ziwich & His International Sound Machine. The "Sound Machine," as far as I can tell, is simply a preprogrammed beat box, but it complements one of the meanest accordions and sharpest pairs of lederhosen this side of Lake Erie. Fred is absolutely tearing it up this afternoon at the new Hofbräuhaus beer hall, getting the entire crowd up on its feet and swinging steins, to polkas and beer chants straight out of the Old Country. A nice Sunday alternative to watching the Browns get creamed yet again while chugging back cans of the standard macrobrew, and a pretty good reason to visit my own hometown.

There is, however, something deliciously atavistic about the whole phenomenon. Because while the Cleveland Hofbräuhaus does indeed feel "new" to the scene (there was an older, unlicensed Hofbräuhaus I remember from my teenage years that had no qualms serving underage imbibers, although it closed years ago), one can't help but feel a twinge of déjà vu. For Cleveland, like many midwestern cities, has had Germans, German beer, and German beer halls from nearly the get-go. Most of what we have traditionally considered "American" beer—Budweiser, Busch, Pabst, Miller—began in these cities a century and a half ago, in beer halls and breweries not so very different from the one I find myself in today. Over the years, the accordian ditties may have morphed into Bob Seger tracks, and the wide variety of German brew recipes may have evolved into the standard pale lagers that citizens now consume by the metric ton, but there's no denying the European origins. Our favorite macrobrews might feel as American as apple pie in this day and age, but the fact of the matter is, they have an exceedingly Teutonic pedigree. At some point in the nineteenth century, what was generally considered to constitute American beer switched from the darker and more fragrant British-style brews produced in New York and Philadelphia to a milder and more refreshing German-style lager brewed largely in the industrial cities of the Middle West.

When Germans began immigrating in large numbers in the mid-1800s, they didn't just bring a new style of beer; they brought a new drinking attitude as well. "It's a social lubricant that's always going to be there," Josh Jones, the brewmaster at the Cleveland Hofbräuhaus, told me. "At a place like this, you'll sit next to complete strangers, and by the end, you'll be friends." *Gemütlichkeit,* as it's known in the Old Country, is the idea that the consumption of beer is a happy, wholesome, family activity that brings people and communities together—not something furtive and mildly illicit for men to do alone in a bar. This new approach to drinking arrived at the exact time when New World beer was seriously waning, and Americans across the social spectrum were binging on the cheap whiskey that poured in from the trans-Appalachian frontier.

But there was certainly more to it than just a happy-go-lucky attitude surrounding the consumption of beer. Indeed, that fun-in-the-sun beer-garden approach belies just how seriously Germans took their beer, and still do today. When Josh moved to the Cleveland Hofbräuhaus from his earlier position at the Great Lakes Brewery, he not only had to be approved by the local franchise owners, but also vetted following a lengthy background check by the regional Bavarian government. Inspectors still come from Germany every few months to check on the brewery, and they take samples back with them to test in their lab. "Fifty percent of brewing is cleaning," Josh informed me, and to that end, his overseers in the old country insist that everything be spotless, and the ingredients pure as can be. This isn't a modern phenomenon; the standards they use go back to the *Rheinheitsgebot,* better known as the German Purity Laws, which haven't changed much in five hundred years. At the Cleveland Hofbräuhaus, Josh Jones follows the same rules German brewers did half a millennium ago. The results, as I and the many others swinging steins to Fred Ziwich & His International Sound Machine can attest, are just as delicious. Good beer translates into good times, and nobody knows this better than the Germans. "The moment when you look out and see everyone enjoying your beer," Josh told me while discussing the rigorous standards and meticulous nature of German brewing, "that's what makes it all worthwhile."

So that's the short version. Now that Fred's taking a break between sets and a fresh mug of Bavarian-style lager is on its way, there's just enough time for the long one.

The love affair between Germans and their beer is an ancient one indeed—a relationship that transcends recorded history. The word *ale* is thought by some scholars to come from the Proto-Germanic word *aluth,* itself derived from an even earlier and murkier Proto-Indo-European word *alu,* which has connotations of sorcery and intoxication; essentially, of being sacred. A tribe called the Alemanii were recorded as making an annual brew contribution to their temple, indicating a religious connotation to beer that was probably shared across the Germanic world. Julius Caesar himself took note of beer's unique status among the Germans during a foray into northern territory in 57 B.C., writing that "they do not allow wine to be imported among them, since they believe that by it men are made soft and effeminate for the endurance of hardship." No, it was *beer* that the pagan Germans cherished, and unlike the Gauls, who became became expert winemakers, not even interactions with the "civilized" Romans to the south could convince them otherwise. The Germans remained steadfastly "barbarian" and stuck to their beer and rambunctious ways. In the first century A.D., the Roman scholar Tacitus would write of them: "No other people indulges more extravagantly in feasting and hospitality," with beer enabling the festivities. When the Roman Empire collapsed in the fifth century, a stampede of Germanic invaders into the old Roman lands begat a flood of German beer there as well. The early Frankish kings who came to rule parts of Germany and northern Gaul brought their love of brewing right along with them. A physician to King Theodoric would write in the sixth century:

> It is on the whole extremely suitable for all to drink beer . . . since beer which has been well made is excellent in terms of benefits and is reasonable, just like the barley soup which we make in another way. However, it is usually cold.

An early take on *Gemütlichkeit,* perhaps, and also proof that the Germans were enjoying a cold, refreshing beer long before Oktoberfests and decorative steins came into the picture. Although the gradual conversion to Christianity that spread throughout Germanic Europe hindered some of the old pagan practices, beer drinking continued unabated.

In early Frankish monasteries, where grain taxes placed on the peasantry allowed for brewing on a larger scale, beer continued to be consumed in substantial quantities. At the Council of Frankfurt in A.D. 794, Charlemagne sought to consolidate the monasteries and convents he controlled under the single order of Benedict, and he included among his many regulations a rule stating that nuns must drink beer on a regular basis, though wine only on special occasions. A ninth-century plan for the St. Gall monastery, likely drafted by the Bishop of Reichenau, included three separate breweries: one that produced beer for monks, another for distinguished guests, and a third for pilgrims and paupers. It may come as no surprise that the monks' brewery was by far the nicest. At similar Carolingian-era monasteries, both in northern France and Germany proper, monks first began tinkering with hops. In the abbey of Freisingen, Germany, hop gardens were being cultivated for brewing as early as A.D. 860, and archaeological evidence indicates that hops were being used in Haithabu, northern Germany, in the ninth century as well.* With the discovery of the plant's preservative properties, using hops as an additive would become the norm, eventually winning out over the older *gruit* spices previously used to flavor German beer. As detailed previously, with the use of hops, beer became

---

*Brewing histories often list the Hallertau region of southern Germany as the cradle of hop usage. While it is true that hops were grown there from a very early time, and that Hallertau would go on to become the biggest hop-producing region in later years, historical records seem to indicate pretty clearly that large-scale hop brewing began in the monasteries of the north. As we shall see, it became widespread in Bavaria only after it had already become a common practice in the commercial breweries of Hamburg and other cities in the Hanseatic League.

The spread of hops throughout Germany during the medieval period made brewing a more profitable enterprise and encouraged the rise of commercial breweries and taverns.

more consistent and more durable; mass production wasn't far behind.

An early example of the transition from sacred to secular beer making can be found in Bavaria, although it likely predates hopping in the region. As early as 1143, monastic brewers in southern Germany were producing more beer than the monks could consume, and, as a result, they began selling it to their neighbors. Monasteries selling beer became relatively common in Germany, in the north and south, as hopping spread and output grew. With all that potential, some men *not* of the cloth began to take note, and soon, monasteries had competition from purely commercial interests. By the 1200s, many monastic breweries were being surpassed by professional town-based brewers, with the growing urban classes relying on the local brewery down the street for their daily tankards, as opposed to the more remote monasteries in the surrounding countryside.

Access to shipping routes in the north of Germany meant that beer needn't stay local. In coastal towns like Bremen, Wismar, and Hamburg, breweries were producing hopped beer that was plentiful and durable enough to be shipped to more distant markets across northern Europe. Soon these port towns, all members of the Hanseatic League, became the leading export centers for European beer. To keep their edge over competitors, as well as maintain quality control, strict brewing regulations were already in place throughout the port cities of the Hanseatic League by the 1300s. "Hamburg" beer, as northern German beer was generically known, benefited from easy access to the grain belt of the Elbe Valley and the hop fields of the Baltic and became famous across the region, from the Low Countries to England and Scandinavia. By the middle of the fourteenth century, Hamburg alone was producing as many as 25,000,000 liters per year. Dutch beer would eventually catch up and come to rival the Hanseatic brews, as would the beers of Bavaria to the south. But for more than a century, Hamburg beer was *the* beer of northern Europe, and it was taxed and regulated accordingly.

The mass production of hopped beer began in northern Germany, but it didn't stay there. It would travel westward to Holland, northward to England, and eventually to Bavaria to the south. The techniques were brought to the region along the trading routes of the Rhine; by the mid-fifteenth century, hopped beer was already common in southern Germany, with locally made wines and unhopped brews becoming increasingly less so. By the late fifteenth century, Bavaria was beginning to rival even the north in both quality and amounts of beer being produced, with licensed merchants and court-run breweries quickly picking up on and copying the effective techniques of their neighbors to the north. "Bock" beer, a long-standing Bavarian institution, was one such imitation, originally designed to duplicate the smooth, drinkable beers of the Hanseatic town of Einbeck.[*] Among their bag of tricks, northern brewers had an ingenious recipe for exceptionally smooth beer: they used wheat in perfect proportion to barley, to produce a softer, more drinkable beverage. Bavarians attempted to duplicate that smoothness, but they had a hard time getting it just right.

That is, until the sixteenth century. In the middle decades of the 1500s, Bavaria developed an ingenious technique of its own. This was not related to hops, but rather to yeast—an entirely new kind of brewing yeast, the origins of which were to be found in a most unexpected place, thousands of miles away from any Bavarian brewery. To protect this new development, a series of rules and regulations would be introduced alongside it, laws that would eventually give Bavarian brewers a tremendous advantage over the competition. So hold on to your Tyrolean

---

[*]If you buy a bock-style beer today, be it in America or Germany, you're likely to encounter some image of a goat on the label. This began as a playful tip of the cap to the Bavarian dialect, which corrupted the name *Einbeck* into *ein Bock*, the Bavarian word for "billy goat."

hats: lager beer, today the most popular form of beer in the world, is about to be born.

Humans have been brewing beer for thousands of years—exactly how many is difficult to say, but it's safe to presume beer is at least as old as agriculture, and possibly even older. For the vast majority of brewing history, the technique remained surprisingly constant. First, the grain was dampened with water to begin the process of germination, which released enzymes capable of converting starches into sugar. This incipient sprouting was abruptly stopped, though, by some form of heat; in the ancient world, by baking the damp grain into bread, and in more modern times, by use of a kiln. The resulting baked grain, now "malted," was added to water to steep in a primitive mash tun, and then boiled in some form of brew kettle. This sugar-rich wort, if left to cool and ferment, would in some cases turn into a beverage that produced a tickle of alcohol on the palate and left the drinker feeling relaxed, uninhibited, and ready at last for that second order of buffalo wings.

That almost magical process of transformation, from a thick barley soup into honest-to-goodness beer, was something that early brewers mastered, but never completely understood. Without microscopes or cellular biology, how could they? They attributed it to all sorts of things, from divine intervention, to a process of instantaneous fermentation akin to spontaneous generation. But in fact, everything they loved about beer owed its existence to a diminutive wild organism called *Saccharomyces cerevisiae*, better known as "brewer's yeast" or "ale yeast." It is a common creature that can be found floating through the air in most corners of the globe. When presented with natural sugars upon which to feed, it does so dutifully and relentlessly, producing a number of waste products, alcohol and carbon dioxide chief among them. This feisty little yeast prefers warmer temperatures and will float atop almost any sweet liquid, feeding in a great foamy mass until it's had its fill. Brewers eventually learned to reuse left-over yeast sediments they favored, resulting in specific strains that produced different characteristics. They were all techni-cally "ales," though, in that they were dependent on various mutated forms of basic ale yeast. Hops or no hops, they still relied on the same microorganism.

In the early sixteenth century, however—and possibly even earlier—Bavarian brewers began to notice something funny was going on with their beer. Many breweries had long been in the habit of "lagering" beer, that is, storing it in cool caves covered in blocks of ice from nearby rivers and lakes. Before refriger-ation, lagering helped beer condition and keep longer. Begin-ning in the early decades of the 1500s, Bavarian brewers started pulling out a very different sort of product from their lagering caves. The traditional beers they were accustomed to were rich, cloudy, almost fruity things, full of complex flavors we now call *esters*. They were also hard to predict—souring was com-monplace, due to unwelcome bacteria and wild yeast strains,[*] and uneven batch consistency was a brewing fact of life. Hops did some to fix the problem, as did making stronger beers with higher alcohol contents, although not nearly enough. But these new "lager" beers that began turning up in their storage caves had a different character altogether. They were lighter, crisper, more carbonated, *and* more refreshing. And they were far more consistent in their quality—infectious bacteria and wild yeasts

---

[*]Souring, in and of itself, is not always a bad thing. In Belgium in particular, sour beer styles such as lambic and gueuze have always used wild yeast and bacteria strains to produce a delicious, albeit tart drink. However, the same *Lactobacillus* and *Brettan-omyces* used to produce those famous ales can become total batch ruiners when they sneak into the wort uninvited.

didn't like cold weather, but whatever was helping to make this beer apparently did. Essentially, Bavarians had discovered an entirely new kind of beer that was easier to drink and easier to market. Something less like a murky, yeasty Trappist ale, and more akin to a frothy golden pilsner (although to be fair, true pilsner malts were still a few centuries away).

As to when this new cold-fermenting type of beer was discovered, well, it gets a bit tricky. The first mention of a cold-fermenting yeast that stayed on the bottom of the beer rather than floating on the top—the fundamental characteristics of a lager—can be dated to Bavaria in 1420. It's possible this was the first reference to the new yeast, although later mentions of cold-fermenting beer from the early and middle parts of the sixteenth century may be more likely candidates, and for a very compelling reason: this new "lager" yeast that fermented at cold temperatures owed its origins to a very unlikely place. Not to monastery on a Bavarian hillside, not some feudal castle on the edge of Munich, but rather to the chilly pine forests of Patagonia. Yes, Patagonia. As in southern Argentina. It turns out, there's a convenient explanation for how this new lager yeast, known to modern scientists as *Saccharomyces pastorianus,* began to appear in the 1500s, right in the foamy wake of Christopher Columbus. Genetic evidence seems to indicate that its ancestor hitched a ride to Europe from the New World. As to whether it was aboard a ship, on a piece of wood, or in the belly of an insect, it's impossible to say. Amerigo Vespucci claimed to have reached Patagonia in 1502; the captain João de Lisboa may have explored its coastline as well in 1512, and Ferdinand Magellan definitely did so in 1520. All are intriguing candidates for stowaway yeast strains, although we will likely never know for sure. What is certain is that at some point in the first half of the sixteenth century, perhaps even a little before then, a wild South American yeast, able to thrive in the cold, dark woods of Patagonia, ended up crossing the Atlantic to Europe, found its way to Bavaria, created a hybrid strain with the local ale yeast, and began producing an entirely new kind of beer. Quite a voyage for a single-celled organism, to say the least.* And a fine contribution from the Americas to beer history.

Naturally, Bavarian brewers at the time knew none of this. Nor did they need to. All they understood was that when they made beer in colder weather, and left it to condition for a few months in a chilly cave, the product had cleaner flavors and was far more stable than the beer they had been accustomed to drinking. These new beers were no longer conventional ales, which had relied on warm-weather-loving ale yeast, but lagers, an entirely novel form of beer that depended on a new hybrid strain of bottom-fermenting, cold-weather yeast. It didn't take Bavarians long to realize they much preferred the latter—and that they could at last give the beer makers of the Hanseatic League to the north a run for their money.

It was not just taste, though. There were enticing economic reasons for leaning toward lager. In much the same way hops had revolutionized the northern German, Dutch, and English beer industries in the fourteenth and fifteenth centuries, lagers would change the way beer was produced and marketed in southern Germany in the sixteenth. Because fermentation occurred at a colder temperature, it was a far slower and less volatile process. With less chance of bacterial infection, batch consistency and longevity improved immensely. This in turn meant beer could be brewed using

---

*The theory that lager yeast owes its origins to Patagonia comes from genetic research. At present, the wild yeast found there is the only possible candidate for its ancestor. It is theoretically possible, though, that the cold-fermenting yeast owes its origins to some other corner of the globe, to a strain that has yet to be discovered—in which case the theory would have to be amended. But for now, Patagonia looks like the only option.

less grain and fewer hops—the high alcohol and hop content needed to brew a consistent, durable ale were no longer necessary. A new dichotomy in German brewing emerged. It was no longer between unhopped ales versus hopped beer, as had been the case in fifteenth-century England, but rather a preference between brews made from traditional ale yeast, be they hopped or unhopped, and those made with the new strains of lager yeast. The age of ales versus lagers had officially begun, and the argument continues to rage to this very day.

For the feudal lords and minor nobility who held sway in southern Germany at that time, though, there was little room for debate. Thanks to their court-owned *Hofbräuhauses,* not to mention the franchise rights and licenses they granted to privately owned breweries and taverns, they had quite a bit riding on the success of the beer industry. They would do anything they could to make it more consistently profitable, including passing all manner of strict regulations and unbending mandates. And lager beer, with its lower costs and higher consistency, was most profitable of all.

Now, the German love of efficiency and quality was applied to brewing long before lager yeast came onto the scene. Charlemagne was enforcing beer quality tests and mandating that brewers keep a clean shop as early as the eighth century in German lands. In the age before hops, the Carolingian kings kept careful tabs on the industry by granting *gruitrecht,* or the right to make beer with *gruit* spices, only to monasteries and towns whose methods and funds they trusted. In Augsburg, Emperor Frederick I was incorporating punishments for unskilled brewers into the city's municipal code as early as 1156, and in Munich, the Duke of Bavaria was only giving brewing licenses to skilled, experienced brewers who produced a consistent product way back in 1286. There are lofty explanations for this early commitment to brewing excellence, but the more practical truth is that brewing was big business and quality mattered. A bad batch of beer was not only detrimental to a local brewery's reputation: it cut directly into the pockets of the nobility, who garnered tremendous amounts of wealth from breweries through taxes and licensing.

The widespread use of hops, which occured in Bavaria roughly a century before lager yeast came into the picture, was most likely the impetus behind the most famous piece of German brewing legislature, the *Rheinheitsgebot,* the aforementioned "German Purity Law." An early version was passed by the Munich city council in 1447 and reissued again in 1487 by Albert IV, Duke of Bavaria. It stipulated that only three ingredients—water, malted barley, and hops—could be used in the production of beer. In an age when many local German brewers were still using all manner of grains and wild (and largely ineffectual) preservative agents to make their beer, it was a way of ensuring that best practices were adhered to, and, incidentally, of ensuring other grains like wheat would always be available to make bread. After all, no one wanted a peasant revolt. A more official, wider-reaching version was signed into effect on April 23, 1516, drafted by the coruling Bavarian dukes Wilhem IV and Ludwig X. Some of it regarded price controls, but it once again mandated that only water, barley, and hops could be used.

This established once and for all the ingredient portion of the law, but it didn't end there. In the decades to come, additional amendments would appear in local brewing codes, albeit with a decidedly different slant. For while the original *Rheinheitsgebot* did serve to regulate what went into beer, in the middle of the sixteenth century, rules were put into play dictating how and when beer was made. In 1551, ordinances were passed in Munich that clearly identified a distinct cold-fermenting style of beer, indicating at last the officially acknowledged arrival of lager yeast on the scene. This was followed up by a 1553 law banning brewing altogether during the warmer months of the year. Why such drastic measures? To ensure that only the longer-lasting, crisper-tasting, and more cost-efficient lager style of beer would be made. The Bavarian brewing season became officially restricted to the time between St. Michael's Day (September 29) and St. George's Day (April 23). With the enforcement of that official calendar, Bavaria's adoption of lager beer became official as well. Thanks to a windblown yeast strain from the forests of Argentina, a schism had formed in Germany—not between the Catholic Church and the northern Reformation, although Martin Luther himself would state that he preferred to "drink a tankard of beer against the devil." But rather, between the ale-sipping north and the lager-chugging south. Bavaria had at last found its own way to compete with the large, commercial breweries of the Hanseatic League. It would brew only lager, a beer whose quality and drinkability surpassed the brews from the north, and whose costs they could far more easily manage.

For the most part, it worked. The Hanseatic League dissolved by the year 1669, and although beer would continue to be made there, its brewing industry was in a state of serious stagnation. Bavarian brewing, meanwhile, was thriving and had no qualms filling the beer vacuum with its own regional lagers. Long gone were the days when the best beer had to be imported from the north—some of the finest beer in Europe was being brewed by the many commercial breweries licensed by the southern nobility. By 1750, Bavaria had some four thousand breweries turning out lager—more than we have in all of America today, despite their having only a small fraction of our current population. The large number of breweries was due in part to local antimonopoly laws that protected the small, private brewhouses in each hamlet or village from "foreign" competition. Essentially, it was in many cases against the law to consume beer from another town, even if it was available and preferred. These protectionist policies came to a screeching halt in the early 1800s, though, thanks to a belligerent Corsican named Napoleon. When France briefly took control of what had been the Holy Roman Empire comprising much of the German heartland, one of his first orders was to ban local groups that might challenge his authority, including brewers' guilds and trade organizations—a move that would effectively kill most protectionist beer legislation across German lands. Napoleon would eventually catch that ferry to Elba and have his Waterloo, but a select and powerful few had made a killing in the new economy, and the free-market approach to German beer was there to stay. Successful breweries either absorbed their competition, or drove them out of business—an age of brewery consolidation had begun. In the Bavarian capital of Munich in 1790, there were sixty breweries in the city proper. By 1819, that number had fallen to thirty-five, and by 1865, it stood at less than fifteen.

There was of course a negative side to Bavarian hegemony and the gradual consolidation of breweries. For several centuries—beginning with the collapse of the northern Hanseatic brewing powers in the 1600s—the southern German duchy could quite accurately have been called a beery bully. Bavarian breweries and the nobles who profited from them used all their influence to spread their *Rheinheitsgebot* to neighboring German states and effectively steal their milk money, or *beer* money as it were (in fact, the universal adoption of the purity laws would even go on to become a Bavarian precondition for German unification in 1871). Again, there probably was an element to quality control, but there also was a far larger impetus to simply knock the competition right out of existence and keep the local Bavarian industry strong. Gradually, over the course of centuries, beloved regional German ales succumbed to the pressure and went the way of the dodo. Even wheat beer was banned for some time, as it wasn't brewed using only malted barley. Fortunately for those of us who love a good Hefeweizen on a hot summer day, the nobility eventually deemed wheat beer too profitable to go extinct, and it was allowed as something of an exception. In addition to Hefeweizen, a few other regional German ales would survive the *Rheinheitsgebot* by the skin of their teeth and persist into the present day—styles you can still find on the import shelves, with names like gose, kölsch, altbier, and Berlinerwiesse. But generally speaking, the vast majority of German ales slowly slipped into the pages of history when they failed to comply with the strict rules set forth by the Bavarian nobility and their powerful breweries. In their place, though, new forms of lager beer evolved to fill in the gaps. Bock, doppelbock, Märzen, and eventually pilsner— the precursor of American pale lager—were born during the heyday of the Bavarian brewing era, each using various malts and techniques to achieve a distinctive character and flavor.

There was another obvious benefit to the eventual predominance of the *Rheinheitsgebot* and subsequent brewery consolidation as well: the larger German breweries that persisted into the nineteenth century did well because they consistently made very good lager beer. A few key technological innovations helped. Thanks to the invention of the microscope in the seventeenth century, science had disproven the theory of spontaneous generation and begun to understand the reproductive process of yeasts. The first usable thermometers arrived in the eighteenth century, meaning the heating of liquids was no longer a haphazard process of guessing. And thanks to a French chemist named Antoine-Laurent Lavoisier, a scientific explanation for the process of fermentation was at last available by 1789. For years, brewers had regarded their

The concept of *Gemütlichkeit* goes back a long way in German culture. Here, three students practice their most sentimental Teutonic tunes over steins of local lager.

craft with awe and wonder; they mastered it, but they did not understand it. At the turn of the nineteenth century, however, science was truly beginning to furnish them with the answers to those ancient mysteries. By the mid-1800s, massive, ultracompetitive lager breweries had become entrenched in Germany, where quality control was carefully monitored by highly trained experts, and scientific innovations were readily adopted for the good of the beer.

All the above paved the way quite nicely for a move to America. The winds had brought lager yeast from the New World aboard European sailing ships in the mid-sixteenth century and transformed German brewing forever. Three hundred years later, a fresh tide of German immigrant brewers took that same yeast back across the sea to America. So, get out that accordion and strike up the oompah band—Herren Busch, Pabst, and Schlitz are all on their way.

As early as 1710, a group of "Poor Palatines" from the southwest of Germany arrived in the Hudson Valley, fleeing the ravages of Franco-Germanic warfare back home. Their establishment in New York encouraged further bursts of immigration from the Palatine region of Germany over the next century, for a mixture of religious and economic reasons. Some stayed in New York, others ventured to New Jersey, and eventually, a considerable number found their way to Pennsylvania. In Philadelphia, they would create one of the first "Germantowns" in America, while in the untamed interior of Penn's Woods, they would either meld with the whiskey-drinking Scots-Irish settlers,* or keep to themselves in rural, oftentimes religiously inclined enclaves, becoming some form of Pennsylvania Dutch. Many of these early German immigrants did drink beer, but not enough to greatly affect the entrenched brewing traditions of early America. Most of the

---

*In fact, America owes its bestselling bourbon to just such a fellow. Jim Beam Inc. can trace its origins to an eighteenth-century German immigrant named Johannes Böhm, who set up a still in the wilds of Kentucky.

Founded in 1829, Yuengling isn't just the oldest existing beer brand in America. It also happens to be the rare example of a German American label that can trace its origins to the first wave of Palatine immigrants, before the second wave of German immigrants arrived in 1848.

first-wave Palatines lacked the resources and expertise to establish commercial breweries of their own and readily adapted to the culture of English-style ales and porters.

There were some exceptions, though, one of which still exists today. Yuengling beer, the long-treasured drink of eastern Pennsylvanians, was started by an ambitious German from the outskirts of Stuttgart named David Gottlob Jüngling. As the son of a relatively successful brewer back in Germany, he came to America better equipped than most of his fellow immigrants to get a brewery off the ground. Following a quickly anglicized name change and some fund-raising, he established the Eagle Brewery in Pottsville, Pennsylvania, in 1829, which almost certainly began by producing ale. The name of the brewery would change when his son came on board, and it eventually made the switch to brewing German-style lager. But its place in the region was there to stay, buoyed along by the beer-thirsty laborers who liked to finish their shift back then, as they still do today, with a nice, cold Yuengling.

For the most part, though, the beer early Germans consumed in America was not lager, the preferred drink from back home. Making it properly required an elusive yeast strain, expansive lagering caves, and a steady supply of ice—none of which was readily available to the humble German farmers and small-time brewers of the late eighteenth and early nineteenth centuries. Nor was there sufficient demand. Most Germans probably weren't thrilled with the beer options set before them, but what other choice did they have? America at that time was dominated by ale breweries. The diary entry of an immigrant and brewer named George Herancourt from 1830 gives some idea of how many Germans reacted upon arriving in their new country:

> In an inn we had 2 or 3 bottles of porter, in America there is not too much good stuff to drink . . . Ale and porter are the best kind of the five sorts they have here . . . I was told that there were 20 breweries in Philadelphia, I went to all of them and could not find work anywhere. Here, you don't have to be a trained brewer; the main thing is, can you work.

From George's account, the situation is clear: comparatively mediocre ales and porters dominated the scene, and brewing them was not necessarily considered skilled labor, the way it had been back in Germany. In the Old Country, George would have been part of a highly trained workforce, beholden to a strict set of state-enforced brewing regulations, and able to turn out a wide variety of delicious, expertly crafted lager

Perhaps the most important beer innovation Germans brought to America was the lagering cellar. This one was dug in Jefferson County, Missouri, in 1859. The beer that cellars like these produced would change the American brewing industry forever.

beers. In Philadelphia, which along with New York was one of the great brew capitals of America at that time, he found his options were limited to a few heavy, murky, often-soured ales, and that his training as a brewer counted for very little. Not exactly *Gemütlichkeit*, to say the least.

But it wasn't all gloom and doom for George and his ilk. Just ten years later, a Philadelphia brewer named John Wagner, who likely brought over a bottom-fermenting yeast strain from Bavaria, began experimenting with lager beers in the cellar under his house. Five years after that, the brewers Charles C. Wolf and Charles Engel created some of the city's first true lagering cellars, allowing a community of homesick immigrants to finally savor beer the way they remembered it in the *gasthauses* and *biergartens* back home. And just across the Alleghenies, in the relatively unsettled region that would come to be known as the Midwest, there were no limits or boundaries to what an ambitious German brewer might accomplish. Tellingly, George Herancourt eventually gave up on finding a job in Philadelphia and started a new brewery of his own in Cincinnati, Ohio. Fortuitously for him, by the late 1840s the floodgates on German immigration were just beginning to open, sending Teutons by the thousands pouring into America's new heartland, to establish farms, found cities, and most important for our purposes, build breweries, ushering in a whole new age of American beer. Whiskey and ale were on the wane; German-style lagers were about to blow them both right out of the water.

To understand why so many Germans suddenly decided to leave behind their homeland for America after 1848, it's crucial to recognize a surprising fact: at this time, they weren't really Germans. While large European nation-states like France, Spain, and England had long since emerged from the feudal chaos of the Middle Ages, the lands comprising modern Germany were still up to their dirndls in it. There was no single consolidated country, but rather a loose confederation of squabbling, autocratic princedoms and duchies that hadn't changed much since the early days of the Holy Roman Empire. And the growing urban middle class— bourgeois merchants, independent tradesmen, freethinking intellectuals—found notions of Divine Right antiquated, if not flat-out repugnant. Essentially, the social reality of the German states was outgrowing its political structure. Charlemagne was long gone, but the modern, progressive-minded burghers found themselves obliged to bend a knee to their clueless kings. They were still stuck with tithes and tributes, in an age when democracy and national identity were becoming all the rage.

These "Forty-Eighters," as they would come to be known, believed in liberal ideals and a common German identity. They wanted a democratic, secular state that incorporated their local affiliation, be it Prussian, Bavarian, Westphalian, or Hessian. The U.S. senator Carl Schurz, who was right in the thick of things back in Germany in the 1840s, would recall: "We young people [believed] that the disintegrated Fatherland must be molded into a united empire with free political institutions. The fermenting, restless spirit permeating the minds of the educated classes, and finding expression in the literature of the day, aroused in us boys the warmest enthusiasm." Individual rights, democratically elected leaders, universal education—such things may not sound terribly revolutionary in hindsight, but at the time, these ideas were nothing short of a powder keg.

And in February of 1848, that powder keg finally exploded. Spurred on by the general unrest that gripped much of Europe at that time, particularly across the border in France, the disgruntled men and women of the confederated German states began to revolt, rising up against the nobles and monarchs in a show of defiance. Protests were organized, marches ensued, and in some cases, even a few weapons were brandished. The liberal nationalists were making a stand, demanding the creation of a modern German republic.

The monarchs did listen—at least, at first. In March of 1848, they conceded to the creation of an elected parliament in Frankfurt. But whatever celebrations the liberal nationalists felt upon that allowance proved to be short-lived. The Frankfurt Assembly, created from a hodgepodge of competing regional and class-based interests, failed to reach consensus as a governing body. When the ruling monarchs of the German states came around to the fact that the assembly could hardly agree on its own name, let alone unite to meaningfully challenge their authority, they gave one another a round of high fives, dissolved the assembly with the help of some aristocratic friends, and effectively crushed the revolution. Some of its participants were in danger of prosecution for treason, others faced retaliatory discrimination, and all were highly disillusioned with the state of things in old Europe. Suddenly, America began to sound like a very tempting alternative. By 1848, German-born Americans already numbered about half a million, scattered mostly across New York, Pennsylvania, and some of the younger states in the country's interior. Those German Americans seemed to be doing just fine. All across what would *eventually* come to comprise a German nation, emigrants began packing their bags by the thousands.

Just how many would come to America? Between 1840 and 1860, over 1,350,000 citizens of German states would arrive in the United States. And because so many of these immigrants were political refugees as opposed to economic ones, they landed on these shores far better equipped than many of their European brethren. They generally had liquid assets and marketable skills from the start. Unlike many other immigrant groups, the Forty-Eighters were already largely middle class upon their arrival, and they fared well in America as a result.

Not that it was *all* beer and skittles. While some did find comfortable homes in eastern cities—by 1855, only Vienna and Berlin had larger German-speaking populations than New York City—many more encountered the same limited opportunities our old friend Charles Herancourt did upon arriving in Philadelphia back in 1830. Just like him, they kept going west, to a part of the nation's interior that would come to be known as the German Triangle, with Cincinnati, Milwaukee, and St. Louis as its vertices. The "Teutonic tide," one historian dubbed it. In 1833, the German population of St. Louis stood at sixteen families. By 1857, one-quarter of the city's 161,000 residents was *Deutsch* in both language and habits. An editorial published in a St. Louis newspaper that same year described the cultural deluge:

> A sudden and almost unexpected wave of emigration swept over us, and we found the town inundated with breweries, beer houses, sausage shops, Apollo gardens, Sunday concerts, Swiss cheese and Holland herrings. We found it almost necessary to learn the German language before we could ride in an omnibus, or buy a pair of breeches, and absolutely necessary to drink a beer at a Sunday concert.

This account, which seems to capture quite nicely the mix of wonder and dismay that Anglo-Americans felt upon encountering this sudden burst of foreign immigration, also hints at the social changes the immigrants initiated. First, the Germans drank and entertained on Sundays—a practice the more puritanical, Sabbath-observing Americans had long refrained from. They liked to do so in beer gardens, a Bavarian tradition that had become popular during the prosperity of the early nineteenth century, based on the notion that it was far more pleasant to drink outdoors under linden trees than indoors in a stuffy saloon. Rather than glasses, they much preferred "steins"—the salt-glazed stoneware kept the beer cool, and the flip-top lid kept the bugs and branches out.* Food was also changing, with frankfurters,

---

*Traditional beer steins may have come from Germany, but so did their downfall. The arrival of *kräusening* and filtration from the Old Country made a more clarified, visually appealing beer possible, and glass quickly replaced the old stoneware mugs so drinkers could appreciate all those golden bubbles.

FRESH COOL LAGER BEER

NEW YORK, PUBLISHED BY CURRIER & IVES, 115 NASSAU ST.

After having to make do with tepid, murky ales that were unreliable and often sour, Americans across the board welcomed crisp, refreshing lager beer with open arms—although some other aspects of German culture took a little getting used to.

Hamburg steaks, and pretzels making their first appearances on street corners, German snacks that Americans today take for granted. And most important, there was the beer itself . . . the breweries, the beer gardens, the brew-soaked *Gemütlichkeit*. A mere decade after the great exodus of 1848, the city of St. Louis could boast close to forty breweries, most of which were German American, churning out more than sixty thousand barrels of lager a year. Germans were transforming the culture of the Midwest, and German beer was playing an inordinately large part.

Following the failed revolutions of 1848, and the subsequent tide of German refugees, a new sight began to appear in many midwestern cities: the beer garden—a far cry from the smoky, all-male taverns and saloons that Anglo-Americans were accustomed to.

This is not to say that beer did not exist in the Midwest before the arrival of Germans. It most certainly did. According to some accounts, the Iroquois were brewing a mildly alcohol beverage from the sweet sap of sugar maples long before Mrs. Butterworth came to town. So sacred was the sugar maple, the Iroquois had their own form of thanksgiving ceremony dedicated to it, and they venerated the trees with ceremonial fires and offerings of incense and tobacco.

The motley collection of French fur trappers and traders who settled the region also brewed. It's easy to forget the Gallic love of beer, given their reputation for viniculture, but it was precious to the French centuries before the arrival of Roman vineyards. Beer never faded in popularity in the monasteries of the north, where Frankish monks would go on to refine the use of hops and facilitate its spread through Germany and the rest of Europe. It was only logical, then, that when French missionaries traveled into the colder, damper parts of the northern Mississippi, they resorted to what they knew how to make best in such places: beer. As one early visitor to French Illinois noted, "Wheat and Indian Corn grow very well . . . their beer is very good." In Kaskaskia, Jesuits had established a frontier mission by the 1760s that consisted of "two hundred and forty *arpents* of cultivated land, a very good stock of cattle, and a brewery." A brewer named François Colman was turning out cold ones for fur trappers and river men in the Missouri settlement of Ste. Genevieve as early as 1779, and Jacques Delassus de St. Vrain was advertising that he had "erected a manufactory and taken into partnership an experienced European brewer" in St. Louis by 1810. His brewery would later change owners, but its genesis was entirely French.

Among them of course were the more traditional Anglo-American and Palatine brewers who came from the East with their ales and porters as well. A Davis Embree was already brewing both in Cincinnati as early as 1810, and even shipping some of his excess downriver to New Orleans. By 1832, a Cleveland newspaper was advertising both ale and table beer, with the local beer trade soon to be dominated by a brewer in the Flats part of town named John M. Hughes, whose "Hughes Ale" would become a local favorite. Detroit followed suit in 1836, when "a single brewery upon the River road" owned by Emerson, Davis & Moore began selling suds, and Chicago beer took off that same year, when the city's first mayor, William B. Ogden, took over the city's primary brewery and turned it into what would become one of the largest in "the West."

With the surge of German immigration in the 1840s and 1850s, all this would change. In fact, the very social and cultural dynamics of an entire region were changing. In 1830, just 5 percent of the population of Cincinnati was German; by 1850, that number had climbed to 27 percent, and a neighborhood called "Over the Rhine" became the city's German cultural center. In Milwaukee, perhaps the most "German" American city of them all, as many as 1,200 immigrants were arriving *weekly* in the wake of the 1848 revolutions, and by 1859, they made up one-third of the city's population. With these hopeful immigrants came a host of musical, political, architectural, and culinary traditions, but perhaps most important of all, they brought a distinctive appreciation for lager beer. To them, beer was not a casual by-product of grain farming. It was not a convenient table beverage or a caloric supplement. To the Germans who poured into the nation's middle, beer was nothing short of a sacrament and an art form. They brought from the towns of Bavaria and the villages of the Rhineland the same appreciation for beer that had guided their forefathers. They wasted no time in replacing the haphazard ale-based brewing culture they found in the Midwest with the more meticulous and artisanal lager traditions they had cultivated back home.

Now, it would be a self-serving exaggeration to say it was beer that brought the Germans to the Midwest—an availability of farmland, a lack of professional competition, and a similarity of landscape and climate all factored into the decision many immigrants made to not stop on the coast, but rather keep plowing west. It would not be hyperbole, though, to state that for a people whose social and cultural life revolved around beer, ease of brewing was certainly a consideration. First, there was the access to grain—the region was well on its way to becoming the buckle in the American grain belt, and in addition to the corn and wheat that fared so well, barley and hops would also thrive, particularly in the cooler north. And thanks to the southward-flowing Mississippi, getting access to grains, especially in a relatively downriver town like St. Louis, was becoming easier by the year. Second, there was the availability of ice. In the days before refrigeration, tremendous quantities of ice were required to keep lager beer cool while it conditioned and prior to serving. Fortunately for brewers, the Great Lakes and their various tributaries were flush with ice, thanks to the region's severe winters and relatively mild springs.

Last, there was the simple question of space. Founding a lager brewery required a lagering cellar or cave of some kind, where barrels of beer could be stored underground for weeks on end. Put quite simply, people back east were running out of room. Cramped quarters and commercial lager brewing simply did not mix, and problems inevitably ensued—sometimes, with comical results, as in the experience of some very surprised Pennsylvania oil prospectors from 1881:

> At a depth of a few hundred feet unexpectedly found what was supposed to be oil; the bailer was run several times and brought up a liquid resembling oil in color, but which was discovered to be beer; it was soon ascertained that the well had been located directly over the storage vault of Grossman's brewery, and that the drill had penetrated the vault filled with beer; the vault had been dug out of the solid rock and extended back into the hill for over 100 feet, the brewery being on the opposite side of French Creek, at the foot of South Park street.

This passage not only illustrates how much darker German American lager was in the nineteenth century—dark enough to be confused with oil—but also how cramped eastern brewing quarters had become. Lagering demanded subterranean real estate that was hard to come by in urban centers—a problem that the relatively undeveloped towns of the Midwest solved quite nicely. Unlike in the East, where the urban landscape was already cluttered by two centuries of settlement, midwestern states like Ohio, Illinois, Missouri, and Wisconsin were still something of an open frontier in the mid-1800s. It was not hard to get the land necessary to build a brewery and dig a lagering cellar, and more than a few of the German newcomers did. By the end of the nineteenth century, the brewing complex of Adolphus Busch would take up a full *seventy* acres of St. Louis riverfront—a feat that would have been tough to duplicate in downtown New York or Philadelphia.

This isn't to say these goliath breweries sprang up overnight. The first German American breweries in midwestern cities were comparatively modest affairs. The brewery of Jacob Best, which would grow into the behemoth Pabst Brewing Company, began in Milwaukee in 1844 as a humble one-story structure on Chestnut Street, squirting out a meager three hundred barrels a year. In 1855, long before "Miller Time" was a national call to action, the Milwaukee brewer Friedrich Müller was also only able to supply roughly three hundred barrels from his simple clapboard brewery along the Plank Road. Keep in mind, this was a man who came to America from a prosperous brewing business in Germany with $10,000 in his pocket—not exactly a "poor immigrant" by any stretch. Even the brewery of the Bavarian newcomer August Krug, which would one day become the gargantuan Joseph Schlitz Brewing Company, was only able to lager some four hundred barrels of beer its first year, following its founding in 1849. Corporate giants, these early brewing companies were most certainly not.

German immigrants brought more than simple lager—they brought a host of distinctive lager styles, including dark, rich bock beer. A lighter, more refreshing pilsner style would win out in the end, however, and ultimately go on to define American beer for most of the twentieth century.

But ambitious, yes, they were. Call it the American dream. Ever industrious and expanding, the first cohort of lager brewers grew their facilities and their output as quickly as their means allowed. Friedrich Müller didn't just change his name to Fred Miller upon settling in America—he updated his entire production apparatus, creating an extensive network of lagering cellars, dug by hand and lined with bricks and limestone, which could condition up to fifteen thousand barrels of beer. And by the 1850s, August Krug had finally teamed up with his own ingenious bookkeeper Joseph Schlitz to form the Krug-Schlitz brewery; the original brewhouse was now an entire brewing compound, complete with a central three-and-a-half-story brick headquarters with double chimneys and parapeted end-walls. German American brewers were on the upswing. As more immigrants and settlers came to the region, their consumer base only grew.

But not all their customers were German. The Irish Potato Famine (the potato itself being a transplant from the Americas) sent a million desperate refuges from the shores of Erin between 1842 and 1852, and a sizable number ended up in American cities. Just like the Germans, many stayed on the coast, but the midwestern capitals received a steady stream of Irish immigrants as well, roughly concurrent with the peak years of the German migrations. Also like the Germans, the Irish were a people with a long-standing tradition of beer. Unlike the Germans, though, the conditions of their arrival did not easily dispose them to brewing. Whereas the former had arrived largely as middle-class political refugees with fungible assets and marketable skills, the Irish were predominantly agricultural laborers from the *Gaeltachts* of the west, running for their lives from the dark specter of starvation. Generally speaking, they came to America with nothing but the shirts on their backs, and in some cases, not even that—a far cry from the ten grand Frederick Miller brought with him on the boat. All of which made it exceedingly difficult to assemble the necessary investments to found a commercial brewery. That didn't mean that a glass of cold beer was unwelcome, and Irish immigrants were among the first non-Germans in America to readily adapt to lager beer. When Irish immigrants did gain the capital necessary to establish their own taverns and restaurants, they often had locally produced German American lager on tap.

By the 1860s, America had developed a taste for lager, bolstered not only by the German American breweries of the Midwest, but by the rising German populations of East Coast cities as well. The Bowery in New York was famous for its beer gardens, some accommodating "from four hundred to twelve hundred guests." German social and athletic clubs called *Turnverein* sprang up not only in cities like Milwaukee and Cincinnati, but in Philadelphia, New York, and Boston as well. As lager breweries began appearing wherever German Americans found a foothold, the older English-style ale breweries fell by the wayside. And just as lager beer had gradually eliminated most of its older ale competition back in Germany, so did it whittle away at its rivals in America as well, for very similar reasons: it was more consistent and stable, it was cheaper to make, and it was generally considered to be crisper and more refreshing. German efficiency and precision had brought a level of quality to American brewing that had been virtually nonexistent before. Tapping a keg of beer was no longer a gamble; you knew you were getting something good. Sour, funky ales and dark, smoky porters were quickly becoming a thing of the past, as Americans came around to the fact that it was indeed "Miller Time" after all.

Between 1840 and 1860, per capita consumption of beer tripled, a feat made possible by an influx of German immigrants and the establishment of their lager breweries. As early as 1856, the *New York Times,* uneasy at the sudden onslaught of immigrant-owned lager breweries, was already warning the nation that lager beer was "getting a good deal too fashionable," with contemporary brewing numbers supporting that claim: In 1850, there had been just 431 breweries in the country, brewing roughly 750,000 barrels of beer. Just a decade later, 1,269 American breweries were producing an annual output of well over a million barrels. Ale and porter were still being made, but the majority of those million-plus barrels would have contained crisp and frothy lager made by upstart German American breweries, which were certainly growing, although not yet huge. By 1866, Milwaukee beer makers were selling over 68,000 barrels of lager, compared to a relatively insignificant output of 3,600 barrels of ale—a sign of the times, and of the inevitable demise of the American ale brewery.

Lager beer did still have one rather imposing rival, and that was whiskey—the fruits of Scots-Irish pioneering and all those amber waves of grain. By the middle of the nineteenth century, America was essentially a whiskey-drinking nation after all, with the hard stuff being far easier to store and transport in what was still a widely dispersed and predominantly rural country. But German lager would get a most unexpected boost beginning on April 12, 1861, when the first shots were fired at Fort Sumter, touching off the American Civil War.

The western expansion that occurred over the course of the nineteenth century proved a boon to the many immigrants and disenfranchised easterners who pointed their wagons toward the setting sun. For many other segments of the American populace, however, this "Manifest Destiny" was nothing short of a disaster. Many Native American societies were either displaced from their traditional lands or destroyed entirely through warfare and disease. Hispanic and Creole settlers from what had been Mexico and French Louisiana often lost whatever position and property their own colonial efforts had won them to the fresh wave of incoming Anglos. For the African American slaves who toiled on southern plantations, western expansion, coupled with the invention of the cotton gin, meant that an institution that had been phased out in the rest of the country was to become not only firmly entrenched, but the rallying cause of southern politicians. With the economies and traditions of southern states so thoroughly tied to the plantation economy, encouraging slavery in the new western territories was necessary to ensure

One Flag — One Country — Zwei Lager.

Even during the Civil War—a conflict in which German Americans from the Midwest played a significant role—both sides could agree on a nice, cold beer.

an equal balance of pro-slavery states. As long as slave states were added in equal measure to the free, the cruelest of American institutions could not be voted out of existence.

The American Civil War was born of this tragedy, dividing families, splitting allegiances, and cleaving a nation. While many recent immigrants were understandably ambivalent about going to war for a nation they hardly knew, German Americans generally supported the Union and rallied to preserve it. There are obvious geographic reasons for this—there were not nearly as many Germans in the South—but cultural and historical explanations as well. The Forty-Eighters had been ousted from Europe based on their own political desire to create a solid union from a mass of querulous German states, and they were generally progressive and liberal leaning in their ideology. As such, they became a tremendous asset to the federal war effort. German language newspapers, like the Milwaukee *Atlas,* supported abolitionist causes and demanded to know why "a lighter colored people had the right to rob darker colored people of their human rights." German American activists lobbied for universal rights and suffrage, declaring as one Carl Schurz did during a speech to Boston Republicans in 1859, that the United States was "the *great colony of free humanity,* which has not old England alone, but the *world,* for its mother country." When it came to practicing what they preached, German Americans by and large did what they could to help abolish slavery and win the war. They put their own sons on the front lines, and they added much-needed funds to government coffers. And although it was certainly unintentional, German lager would benefit from the war as well.

Close to a quarter of all northern troops—half a million men—came from immigrant backgrounds, and of these, more than two hundred thousand were born in Germany. Many midwestern regiments consisted entirely of German Americans, such as the Ninth Ohio, Ninth Wisconsin, and Thirty-Second Indiana. The Turners, a German political organization that lent their name to the *Turnverein* clubs, worked as Lincoln's bodyguards at his inauguration in 1861, as the group had proven instrumental in rallying German Americans to vote for Honest Abe. With all those German troops, as one might expect, came a great thirst for German beer. The old one-quart beer ration of the American Revolution was long gone by that point, but beer was still available to the troops. A *Harper's Weekly* illustration published during the war shows "The Lager Bier Wagon" trundling through the front lines to supply German soldiers, and one brigadier general even suggested the following tongue-in-cheek plan to get the Yankees out of Missouri: "Burn all the breweries and declare Lager Beer to be a contraband of war. By this means, the [Germans] will all die in a week and the Yankees will then run from the state." There was more than a grain of truth in this—to go without beer was unthinkable for most Germans, and they went to great lengths to procure it even during the most trying periods of the war.

Predictably, overindulgence, although frowned upon by the discipline-loving German commanders, was not uncommon either, as demonstrated by the many court martial records of German regiments. A Private Frank Kolb of the First Missouri Horse Artillery celebrated Christmas of 1863 by going on a tremendous beer bender and calling his commanding officers "humbuggers and shit asses." Another private, Jacob Schultz, had at least one beer too many in Paducah, Kentucky, and proceeded to break into a general store and steal a tremendous quantity of envelopes and cigars. A first lieutenant named Louis Hoftsedter became so intoxicated at Jefferson Barracks, he lay on the sidewalk and refused to rise, eventually causing such a row, the king of Bavaria had to send the army a letter on his former subject's behalf. In one of the most amusing incidents of brew-based shenanigans, another first lieutenant and prison guard named Frederick Klentz released a prisoner without orders from a St. Louis stockade, took that prisoner to Jacob Sched's beer hall in town, and bought the man multiple rounds of drinks and cigars. All proof that even in the midst of some of the worst battlefield horrors in history, the Germans still made room for a little *Gemütlichkeit*.

It was the Germans' fiscal contribution that would secure their place—and their beverage—in mainstream American society. Assembling one of the largest armies the world had ever seen to defeat secessionist rebels was an expensive endeavor. To help cover those sudden costs, Washington turned to the same business that had helped fund the Revolution in 1776 and assisted once again in 1812: booze. On July 1, 1862, President Abraham Lincoln signed an Internal Revenue Act into effect that required brewers and distillers to pay fifty dollars for a yearly license, a tax of twenty cents per gallon on spirits, and one dollar for every thirty-one-gallon barrel of lager, ale, and porter.

Distillers—many of whom were based in border states— wrung their hands over the sudden increase in taxes. But the emerging class of German brewers, centered largely in the brewing capitals of the Northeast and the rising cities of the Midwest, saw an opportunity. More than a few of them had been involved in the social and political upheavals that had rocked Germany two decades prior, and they recognized that they would need to be organized to help negotiate these precarious times. It was, after all, the inability to cohere that had cost the Forty-Eighters their unified government, and they wouldn't make this mistake again.

On August 21, 1862, a Forty-Eighter named John R. Katzenmayer, who was a brewer for the firm of A. Schmid & Co. in New York, organized the first meeting of local beer makers. There, they laid the groundwork for a national convention of brewers, and in February of 1863, the first truly national meeting was held, welcoming into the fold the multitude of German brewers from what at the time were considered "western" states. Officially, this new organization—what would become the United States Brewers' Association (USBA)— existed to "attend to the interests of the General Association of Washington." Unofficially, their aim was to do everything they could to further the interests of German American brewers and lager beer. Established ale and porter brewers, who at that point still produced a decent portion of the beer Americans consumed, were not invited to early meetings and were only included later as something of a diplomatic afterthought, once the leadership and hierarchy of the organization was firmly established. The conventions were conducted entirely in German, as were all the early publications. German was declared the official language of the brewers' convention and remained so throughout the 1860s and early 1870s—a fact that still left the Anglo-American brewers of ales and porters largely in the dark as to the subtler points of the organization's meetings even after they were finally invited.

Thanks to the lobbying efforts of the USBA, not to mention sympathetic midwestern politicians, lager brewers were able to convince Washington that not just beer, but *lager* beer, was distinct from other, stronger forms of alcohol, more healthful and wholesome, and ought to be taxed at a far lower rate. The dollar-per-barrel tax was decreased to sixty cents, and tariffs were eventually reduced on imported barley—a raw material brewers deemed necessary to augment their own rationed domestic supply during wartime. Lobbyists for the USBA even managed to make the lager that predated the Revenue Act (still conditioning in cellars across the country) exempt from taxation entirely. They explained to the government that it "might have been possible, at some risk and expense, to remove ale and porter brewed prior to September 1, 1862, yet it was utterly impossible to remove lager beer prior to that date without destroying the article," meaning, of course, lager beer. Lager brewers eventually received a full refund on any taxes they had paid on existing lager beer, while the ale and porter brewers remained on the sidelines, scratching their heads and emptying their pockets. Such a feat of political savvy may seem incredible, but the USBA was adept at demonstrating to politicians the vast amounts of treasure the breweries could provide—assuming they were given the exemptions they needed to thrive. Ultimately, the relationship benefited the government and German brewers alike. Whiskey distillers and ale brewers, who were generally less organized and reluctant to employ expensive lobbying tactics, were essentially left out of the agreement, while the lager brewers knocked back one more drink with Uncle Sam. The lager industry did contribute tremendous sums to the government's war chest, but they did so in a way that proved mutually beneficial to brewers and politicians alike. In exchange for their assistance with the war effort, they found themselves in a unique position. Suddenly, lager beer was no longer an ethnic peculiarity but a force to be reckoned with. A spokesman for the lager brewers, writing with all the acuity of hindsight some thirty years after the war, would state the following:

> Between 1842 and 1863 brewing had developed so rapidly and became so firmly established that it could, doubtless, have held its own ground successfully, even without discriminating legislation; but, on the other hand, it is quite certain that without such legislation it would never have become a national beverage, nor would its progress during the past thirty-five years have been what it actually is. Hence, the introduction of the internal-revenue system really proved a blessing to the trade, not only on this account, but also because it called into existence the United States Brewer's Association.

The North won the war, and the lager brewers won their own place at the American beverage table. The *head* of the table, as a matter of fact. By the time Robert E. Lee finally laid down his saber on April 9, 1865, America was well on its way to becoming a lager-drinking country, and the handful of ale and porter brewers that remained were destined not to last.

A few ale brewers would survive the wartime and postwar industry cull—Newark's famous Ballantine Ale, established way back in 1840, is one such malty coelacanth. But generally speaking, the days of the original Anglo-American ales and porters were over. A tradition that went back to the first seasick Pilgrims who set foot on Plymouth Rock, and that was carried on through the tankards of minutemen and the brimming cups of founding fathers, was destined to be supplanted by a clearer, crisper, more effervescent, and in many cases, more artfully made class of beer. The age of the American lager had begun.

What an age it was. Following an awkward adolescence and the rebellious period of the Civil War, the United States experienced one heck of a growth spurt. In a few decades, America transformed from a relatively inconsequential global bystander into a heavily urbanized, industrial goliath. Between 1850 and 1900, the population of the United States more than tripled, from twenty-three million to seventy-six million. In 1850, a mere 15 percent of people lived in cities; by the century's end, that number was closer to half. In roughly the same time span, petroleum production leaped from less than a million tons to nearly fifty million, and crude steel output went from practically nil to over ten million tons. Immigrants were pouring in as well, attracted by the economic opportunities that all that industry offered. American cities teemed with Germans, Irishmen, Italians, Slavs, and Jews, all looking for labor, all eager to contribute. Much of this thunderous growth took place in the burgeoning capitals of the American Middle West. Midwestern cities were growing to rival the traditional metropolises of the East, and in some instances, even surpassed them. In the 1850 census, of the ten largest American cities, only two were in what is today considered the Midwest—Cincinnati and St. Louis. By the dawn of the twentieth century, half of the ten largest cities would be found in the Midwest, with Chicago second only to New York in total population.

The brewing industry flourished as well. At the end of Civil War, America's entire brewing infrastructure was struggling to turn out a mere three million barrels. By 1900, that number had reached nearly forty million barrels. The increase in per capita consumption was drastic, growing among drinking-age adults from less than six gallons a year, to nearly twenty gallons—a number similar to what Americans on average drink today. In 1850, the brewing industry's total capital was along the lines of four million dollars; in just fifty years, it grew 100-fold. Barley production jumped from around 5 million bushels to almost 180 million bushels in roughly that same time period, and hops went from a measly 6,000 bales in 1840, to over 225,500 bales by the year 1900.

The locus of brewing shifted away from the East. On an individual state basis, New York still led the pack at the close of the century, with powerful brewers like George Ehret churning out the suds—his brewery was the nation's largest in 1877—but the gap was narrowing. St. Louis and Milwaukee both had consolidated breweries that could compete with even the largest on the East Coast, some of which were capable, by the first decade of the twentieth century, of producing over a million gallons a year. This put them up not only with the largest breweries in the country, but the world. And whereas the first conventions of the United States Brewers' Association had been held in New York and Philadelphia, those that followed after the war would reflect the westward shift of American brewing: St. Louis in 1866, Chicago in 1867, and Cleveland in 1873. By the early 1900s, it wasn't even a question—the USBA was a midwestern organization.

Apart from tax breaks, what drove this midwestern beer

revolution? In part, it was the general prosperity that gilded the latter decades of the nineteenth century, and the influx of cheap labor and materials that poured into the region. But we'd be neglectful not to raise our steins to the brewers themselves, and to their accumulated wisdom from centuries of German brewing. In the old German brewing industry, consolidated, state-sanctioned breweries were fiercely competitive, but united as a group when necessary to protect the industry as a whole. While these brewers understood the importance of tradition, they also appreciated the necessity of innovation. Just as their Bavarian and Rhenish forbearers had embraced new yeasts, new brewing techniques, and novel technologies in the centuries prior, the brewers of the Midwest readily adapted—and adopted—when it proved advantageous.

In the second half of the nineteenth century, they made significant changes to the actual character and quality of the beer itself. Most German American brews of that era, even relatively crisp lagers, were significantly darker and richer than the mass-produced lagers of today—more like the bocks and Märzens of the Old Country, and much less like a watery light beer. But in a hardworking, industrializing nation, there was an appetite then, just as there is now, for lighter, more refreshing beers, something to quench the thirst after a long day at the mill. As a result, the breweries of the Midwest were trailblazers in creating what would eventually evolve into the iconic American pale lager. This was possible in part due to advancements in kilning technology that had occurred just prior to the Civil War. The indirect heat kiln enabled malts to be roasted without direct contact with the heat source, and the strong, smoky, slaggy flavors of yore were largely eliminated, to be replaced by the subtler, lighter flavors inherent in the malted grain. Controlling temperature also became an

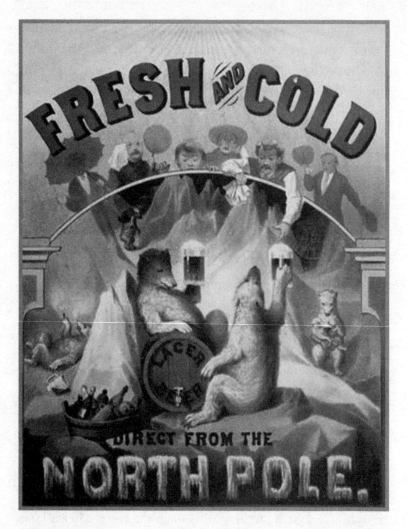

With American beer becoming lighter and more carbonated in the decades that followed the Civil War, the idea of "coldness" was sold along with it. Beer was increasingly sought after as a source of refreshment by what was, by the late nineteenth century, a hardworking and industrialized nation.

exact science—suddenly it was possible to produce far lighter, more enzyme-rich malts, which in turn produced paler, crisper lagers. These advancements had helped to popularize pale, crisp Bohemian-style pilsners all across Europe in the middle of the nineteenth century, and it was a trend that German immigrant brewers would eventually bring to America as well, as soon as they had accumulated the resources to establish malting kilns of their own.

To augment that softness and drinkability even further, midwestern brewers also began to supplement their mash bills with grains other than barley, turning several hundred years of *Rheinheitsgebot* hegemony right on its head. The North American variety of six-row barley commonly used in American malts had a higher enzyme concentration than German two-row barley, which made it easier to throw other adjunct grains into the mix. The adjuncts' primary virtue was price—corn, wheat, and rice from America's widespread grain farms were generally cheaper than fickle northern barley—but they also made for beers with gentler flavor profiles and paler hues than barley malt alone. Budweiser and Schlitz both were early adopters of rice in their grain bills, and corn, the *original* American grain, would become a crucial ingredient in many midwestern lagers, including Miller and Pabst.

The quest for a milder, more drinkable beer was only furthered by a steady decline in alcohol content and hop usage across the industry. Improvements in transport and temperature control—both of which will be covered in short order—made spoilage less of a concern, meaning that the preservative properties of alcohol and hops, which had defined American beer since the beginning, became ancillary in much of the country. A general movement toward lighter, crisper beers that began with the first Bavarian lager innovations of the sixteenth century would be continued and perfected in the American Midwest throughout the late nineteenth and early twentieth centuries, as German American brewers adapted the robust bocks and flavorful pilsners of the Old Country

The painting *Custer's Last Fight,* pitching the Budweiser brand beneath, became one of the American beer industry's first truly national ad campaigns. The painting appeared in taverns and saloons all over the country.

to be drinkable and salable in the New. Paler malts, softer grains, subtler hops, and lower gravities all resulted in an entirely new style of beer, one that was largely German in heritage, but distinctly American in its personality

With a crisp, refreshing product to sell to all those hard-working Americans, brewers also changed the way it was sold. In 1896, long before Spuds MacKenzie or the Bud Bowl took America by storm, Anheuser-Busch launched an early version of an ad campaign by buying the rights to the Cassilly Adams painting *Custer's Last Fight.* Once the rights were procured, the brewery commissioned another artist to paint a smaller, modified version, which featured even more violence and faux gallantry than the original, printed the Anheuser-Busch name across the bottom, and distributed some 150,000 copies of it to every tavern and saloon that sold its signature Budweiser beer. This highly romanticized version of the Battle of Little Bighorn played up to contemporary notions of western expansion, caught the public's attention, and helped spread awareness of the beer, all at the same time. The campaign proved so successful that fifty years later, an estimated one million copies had been printed, and the picture had become, according to one historian, "viewed by a greater number of the lower-browed members of society—and by fewer art critics—than any other picture in American history." Other brands followed Budweiser's example, and the modern era of beer marketing was born. Breweries began owning and sponsoring beer halls and saloons, with the agreement, not entirely unlike that of the old court-licensed beer halls of Bavaria, that only their beer was to be sold to customers. Suddenly, logos and slogans were everywhere, on posters, ashtrays, beer mugs, and pool tables. For the first time, large midwestern breweries were becoming household names.

As profits rose, workers wanted their share. German Americans not only owned and managed many of the Midwest's breweries, but they also tended to its mash tuns, checked up on its brew kettles, put the finished beer into barrels, and transported it to distribution centers. The same liberal spirit of progressive politics and social organization that had bound the Forty-Eighters in a common cause one generation prior made the brewing industry an early example of organized labor in a part of the country that would become famous for it. When steel mills were just getting off the ground, and automobiles not yet a glimmer in Henry Ford's eye, the workers at German breweries were forming industrial unions to protect their rights. According to one report, there were some 2,347 workmen employed by breweries in 1850. By 1880, that number stood at 26,220, more than a tenfold increase. The rapid expansion that the brewing industry had experienced, and hoped to continue experiencing, was contingent on their involvement. Consequently, workers demanded to be compensated fairly. The very earliest attempts at organized labor can be found as far back as the 1850s, when German workers began forming trade associations and mutual aid societies in St. Louis and Cincinnati. In the latter city, workers would form the Brauer Gesellen Union in 1879, lobbying for and eventually winning through boycotts a reduction of the workday and increase in the minimum wage. In 1886, brewery workers formed the National Union of United Brewery Workmen, an almost exclusively German American alliance that held considerable sway in the Midwest for close to a century, until it merged with its longtime rival, the Teamsters Union, in 1973. Happy workers produce good beer, and breweries were generally able to expand their production without the ugly growing pains seen in other, more exploitative industries like coal or steel.

It would be technology, though, that would ultimately pave the way for the massive growth of the midwestern breweries in the late nineteenth and early twentieth centuries. In the decades following the Civil War, the United States experienced a burst of scientific innovation; entire industries were revolutionized, as steam power, electricity, and a host of other new technologies enabled what had essentially been cottage industries to become large-scale, commercial endeavors capable of mass production. Just as their predecessors in Germany had readily adopted microscopes and thermometers, so too did German American brewers incorporate the latest inventions of their day into their brewing regimen. In 1876, the Frenchman Louis Pasteur published *Etudes sur la Bière,* which demonstrated a heating technique for producing beer devoid of contamination. By rapidly bringing the finished liquid to a temperature just below boiling, the process made it possible to store beer for far longer periods of time. When paired with new techniques for filtration and forced carbonation, the result was shelf-stable beer that could be sold crisper, cleaner, and more bubbly than ever. For years, brewers had depended on the technique of *kräusening* to add a champagnelike kick to their beer. It did work, but it also relied on the late addition of active—*and* unreliable—yeast into a fermented brew. With pasteurization, carbonation, and filtration available, suddenly that old Bavarian trick was no longer the only way to get a foamy head on the top of a crystal-clear lager. For better or for worse, the days of volatile, hoppy, sediment-heavy beers were numbered in America. Once again, German American brewers were using the latest techniques to produce a more stable, more clarified, and more drinkable beer—something those who appreciated the complex flavor profiles of traditional lagers surely lamented, but many more celebrated with a lively *Prost*. Pasteurized beer wasn't a "living" thing filled with active yeasts and the occasional bacterium, but a nearly sterile and static product with an extended shelf life.

It didn't stop there. This new, even paler variety of American lager was soon to be served in a whole new way, as improved bottle-making technologies meant that beer no longer had to be transported primarily by the barrel. What had once been a laborious process of blowing and molding had become by the end of the 1800s a far more efficient, mechanized affair. In 1898, the American Owens machine was able to produce a mind-boggling twenty-five hundred glass bottles in an hour—bottles that could readily be filled with a pasteurized, freshly carbonated lager capable of sitting in groceries and taverns for weeks on end.

Basic mechanization, made possible through advancements in steam power, would also do its part in taking an industry whose methods had changed little since the Middle Ages fully into the modern era. Steam engines capable of continuous rotary motion had been known to science since the late eighteenth century; but in the late nineteenth century, industrialists came to recognize their full potential, and German American brewers were certainly no exception. Even as early as 1865, with the nation still reeling from the Civil War, breweries were using steam to render their process more efficient and productive. Steam not only processed grains and moved product—it provided a controlled heat source to boil the wort. The sheer efficacy of this new technology is explained in the following account, regarding a German American brewery from that era:

> The engine is sixteen horse power. It can, at the same time, grind the malt, sift it, throw it into the mash tub, let in boiling water that it has made to boil, stir up the malt and water, draw it off, pump it up stairs and throw it into the kettle, heat the kettle of liquid until it boils, throw it out into the coolers, cool it, force and carry it off into vats, ferment it, chafe it, and draw it off beer. With a little practice the engine could be taught to drink beer.

The steam engine vastly transformed an industry that for hundreds of years had been reliant solely on manpower; steam power made mass production possible, in the brewing industry and many others as well.

Two other recent inventions played perhaps the largest roles, changing what had been a locally consumed product into a national beverage: refrigeration and rail transportation. The first was made possible by improvements in compression-based cooling technology just after the Civil War. The second came to pass when developments in steam power met the catalyst of western expansion. Both would combine to alter the beer industry forever.

As early as 1860, breweries were using an early artificial ether compression refrigeration system made by Jacob Perkins to cool their product. More refined designs followed, and by the late 1870s, the trade publication *The Western Brewer* was already forecasting a revolution in refrigeration was in the making, with ice machines quickly to replace the lagering cellars and natural icehouses that had come before. By 1891, this prediction had proven quite astute, and the same publication announced, "almost every well appointed brewery is refrigerated by machinery, and nobody thinks of questioning their value." German Americans with names like Krausch and Jungenfeld led the field in the development of refrigeration systems and sold them to breweries across the Midwest. Aboveground stock houses became a standard feature of larger breweries, and for the first time, thanks to refrigeration and ice production, brewing lager beer was no longer a seasonal activity, or reliant on environmental ice. With artificial refrigeration, proper temperatures for the production and conditioning of lager beer could be regulated all year round. Suddenly, there was no limit to how much beer an ambitious brewery could turn out, and thanks to pasteurization for bottles and refrigerated storage for barrels, there was also suddenly no rush to sell it.

Distributing it was still a challenge. But it was a challenge that America's emerging rail system would quickly overcome. In truth, functioning steam-engine locomotives had existed since the early nineteenth century. It would not be until after the Civil War, though, during the subsequent industrial boom, that a national railway system would blossom. In 1865, the network of rails in America extended a mere 35,000 miles; by 1870, it had swelled to 53,000. In 1880, roughly 93,000 miles of track were available for shipping, while by 1890, this number had reached 164,000 miles. With all that expansion came a vertiginous drop in shipping costs. In just a few decades, shipping by rail had gone from an expensive and inconvenient way to get goods across the country, to the *only* way. All that freshly laid track didn't just open up new portions of the American frontier—it meant goods could travel quickly and cheaply to almost anywhere in the country. Including, as it were, lager beer. The arrival of *refrigerated* railcars and track-side stock houses suddenly meant there was practically no part of America that was beyond the reach of the larger breweries. New markets were opening up, and local midwestern labels were well on their way to becoming national brands.

The impact of refrigerated railway cars cannot be overstated. They fundamentally changed the brewing and selling of beer. For those who incorporated the new technology, there were untold riches waiting. For those who dawdled or hung their hats on tradition, well, they usually didn't fare so well. As one might expect, the nimble breweries of the Midwest generally fell into the first category. Take Anheuser-Busch, for example. In 1877, the St. Louis brewery produced just 44,961 barrels of beer—it didn't even make it on the top twenty list when it came to American breweries. In the decades that followed, though, the company not only adopted the use of cutting-edge refrigerated train cars, it actually began manufacturing its own. By 1895, it had become the second-largest brewery in America, and in 1901, it was right up there at the top of the list with Pabst and Schlitz, coming out at a whopping one million barrels. Now, compare that to the New York–based Hell Gate Brewery of George Ehret. In 1877, it was the largest producer of beer in the country, putting out 138,449 barrels of beer to thirsty New Yorkers. But Ehret generally eschewed refrigerated railcars, opting instead to stay local. As a result, his brewery had dropped to fourth place by 1895, soon to be surpassed by Anheuser-Busch, Pabst, and Schlitz—all of which were located in the Midwest, and utilized artificial refrigeration and national rail distribution to its fullest potential. With beer now being made year round, and for the first time sold to a truly *national* market, the future for midwestern beer was boundless. The big breweries had nowhere to go but up. On the eve of the twentieth century, they found themselves quenching the thirst of an entire country: beer had once again become the American drink. Not too shabby for a scrappy bunch of German refugees who had come to America a half century before, filled to the brim with hops and dreams.

And they proceeded to do exactly what those with sudden success and riches are told never to do; they let it all go straight to their heads. That first cohort of German American brewers came from a tradition of Rhenish dukes and Bavarian princes using breweries as private piggy banks, so it should come as no great shock that when the bucks really started coming in, they shifted away from the values of the Forty-Eighters and reinvented themselves instead as true beer barons. As the new monarchs of the Middle West, they engaged in acts of ostentation that would put the rest of the Gilded Age crowd to shame.

Take the Prussian-born Frederick Pabst, for example. When the twenty-eight-year-old waiter and part-time steamer pilot purchased a half interest in his father-in-law's failing Milwaukee brewery in 1864, he was hardly what one might consider a captain of industry. By the 1880s, however, he was captaining one of the largest breweries in the country, and spending his vast fortune as boastfully and profligately as one might expect. In 1889, he had created his own Pabst beach resort in Whitefish Bay, capable of entertaining as many as

Built in 1891, the Pabst Building was Milwaukee's first skyscraper, and a visual representation of the power that the city's German American brewers commanded.

ten thousand visitors in a single day. To compete with his rivals, he turned the traditional German beer garden into a rollicking, oompahing spectacle, installing carnival rides, Ferris wheels, concession stands—in effect, creating one of the first truly American mega-amusement parks, all built on beer. His follow-up, Milwaukee's Pabst Park, would complete the transformation from beer garden to amusement park by featuring a roller coaster with fifteen thousand feet of track and a gigantic "Katzenjammer palace" funhouse. As for his famous blue ribbon insignia, the beer never actually won such a prize at any festival; old Fred liked to place a blue ribbon around his "Best Beer"—named, in fact, after his father-in-law, Phillip Best—and let those in attendance draw conclusions for themselves. In 1892, the company bought nearly one million feet of silk ribbon, which Frederick required workers to hand-tie around every bottle of his Best Select. With his vast brewing fortune, he would even go on to buy a German opera house and a stock farm for raising Percheron horses. When he died in 1904, he had the largest brewery in America to his name and had become the wealthiest man in Wisconsin.

Not one to be outdone, Joseph Schlitz was Frederick Pabst's top rival and archnemesis. From his humble beginnings as a brewer's bookkeeper, Joseph eventually took control of his employer's brewery, married the former owner's widow, and became powerful enough to trade punches with the most prominent brewers in the city of Milwaukee. He transformed a little brewery that had once struggled to turn out 150 barrels in a single year into a sprawling industrial complex that spanned eight city blocks. Always the shrewd marketer, Joseph rarely failed to capitalize on world events to promote his famous Milwaukee beer. After the Great Chicago Fire—which destroyed much of the city's brewing infrastructure—he supplied the whole town with free suds, making sure they remembered where that beer was coming from: the Schlitz slogan, "The Beer That Made Milwaukee Famous," would eventually be adopted to capitalize on that act of goodwill. Sadly, Joseph's career at the helm of the brewery was cut short—he died in a shipwreck in 1875 at the age of forty-three—but his bold legacy would live on in the decades that followed.

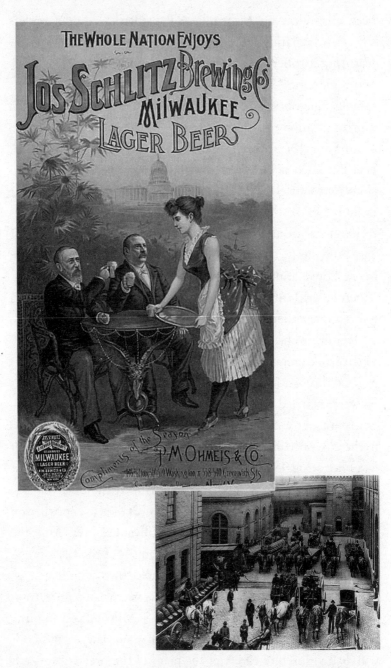

Expanded facilities and a thriving distribution network helped Schlitz beer spread well beyond its home in Milwaukee. But for local deliveries, they still used horses.

One of the most visible symbols of beer baron extravagance was the Schlitz Palm Garden in Milwaukee. Though ostensibly a beer garden, it had little in common with the humble lager patios the first German immigrants had frequented.

To make sure Pabst knew his amusement parks weren't the only ride in town, Joseph's successors created Schlitz Park, complete with a bowling alley and the novelty of "electric lights," as well as the elegant Schlitz Palm Garden, right beside the Schlitz Hotel. When Commodore Dewey and his men captured Manila during the Spanish-American War of 1898, the Schlitz brewery sent thousands of celebratory bottles to the victorious sailors; disapproving temperance societies were told that beer could help stave off the effects of malaria. While Joseph would not live to see it, his brewery would surpass his old archrival Pabst in 1902 with a total output of over one million barrels, making Schlitz the biggest beer brand in Milwaukee, the United States, and, yes, even the world.

As the head of what was to become America's most powerful beer dynasty, Adolphus Busch cultivated a personality that was larger than life—a curious amalgamation of a German nobleman and an American tycoon.

Without a doubt, however, the most grandiose, the most truly baronial of all the midwestern beer barons was the always oversized, always outspoken scion of St. Louis brewing, Adolphus Busch. As a pioneer in both pasteurization and refriger-

The winter residence of Adolphus Busch, in Pasadena, California. Not bad for an immigrant from a little town on the Rhine. Toward the end of his life, the beer baron did engage in philanthropy and donated a considerable portion of his wealth to charitable causes.

ated distribution, the immigrant from Kastel, Germany, had grown his own father-in-law's brewery into a national giant by the time he was in his thirties. With all that success came tremendous amounts of both fame and fortune, and with a personal income estimated at two million dollars a year—an almost unthinkable amount of wealth at a time when average annual salaries were still in the hundreds—Adolphus could afford a little extravagance. He dressed to the nines in richly tailored European finery, and he sported a lavish goatee attended to by his personal manservant and barber. Indeed, so regal was his bearing, even William Howard Taft referred to him as "Prince Adolphus." He built mansions in St. Louis, Pasadena, Cooperstown, and even back in old Germany, on

In just a few decades, Anheuser-Busch went from a relatively small local brewery in St. Louis to the largest producer of beer in the country, opening satellite breweries and shipping its product to towns and cities across America.

the banks of the Rhine. When he built his palatial estate in Pasadena, J. P. Morgan and Andrew Carnegie took note, eventually resulting in the city's "Millionaires' Row," as other industrial titans followed his lead and built houses nearby. The opulence didn't end, though, when Adolphus walked out the door. Thanks to a private railcar capable of pulling right up to his mansion at 1 Busch Place, actually named *The Adolphus,* he could travel the country in unimpeded luxury and inimitable style. Everywhere he went, he championed the cause of his Budweiser beer.

The grand ambitions of the midwestern beer barons, when coupled with the developments in distribution and marketing that were transforming the industry, would eventually allow the unthinkable to occur: the unseating of Germany as the world capital of beer. In 1911, the United States actually knocked the *Vaterland* out of its top position, becoming the largest beer-producing country in the world with a grand total of sixty-three million barrels. To state it simply, America had changed. In half a century, the nation transformed from a whiskey-drenched backwater of small-time farmers to an industrialized, beer-chugging colossus. It had evolved from a former English colony with a handful of ale breweries to a truly distinct nation populated by a host of diverse ethnic groups that liked their lager pale, crisp, and carbonated. And the industry, not to mention its consumer base, only seemed to be growing. What could possibly go wrong?

Well, as it turned out, quite a bit. Not everyone in America was keen on seeing immigrants rise in the ranks, and not all who watched this demographic shift celebrated it with a swinging stein. The slight shock many Anglo-Americans felt upon first encountering Sunday drinking and beery good times in the mid-nineteenth century had fermented by the beginning of the twentieth into flat-out resentment. The sight of German beer barons flaunting their wealth certainly didn't help, but the sinking of the *Lusitania* by German torpedoes in 1915 sealed the deal. Whatever traces of goodwill toward the German American beer industry that remained after World War I were quickly rendered moot by the passing of the Volstead Act. In one of our nation's most shocking bouts of reactionary politics, alcoholic beverages, not to mention the German beer halls, Irish taverns, and Italian wine shops where they were served, were made illegal on January 17, 1920. Overnight, beer went from being a mildly intoxicating staple to a controlled substance that could land you in jail. Prohibition had begun.

Granted, it wouldn't *totally* ruin the industry. A handful of breweries were able to weather the thirteen-year storm by producing soft drinks and malted products, and they would emerge bigger and more consolidated than ever before. American beer would never quite be the same, though. In an effort to turn a profit as quickly as possible after all those years of crippling prohibition, an even paler, more watery product would be developed and mass-produced, to be served up in cans across the country. While it may have helped quench the thirst of a weary worker during the Great Depression, a parched G.I. in the midst of World War II, and even a few hungover coeds on MTV Spring Break, the final product bore only a passing resemblance to the rich and hoppy lagers that German immigrants had first brought to this country.

Although, when you're sitting here in the Cleveland Hofbräuhaus, sipping on a tall *Maß* of dunkel while Frank Ziwich & His International Sound Machine prepare for a second set, you can still get a taste of all that was lost.

Something pretty damn delicious.

Take it away, Frank.

CHAPTER 5

❦

THE WEST

or

Beers of the Wild Frontier

IF THERE'S A PERSON OUT THERE WHO HAS A MORE compelling résumé—not to mention beard—than Indiana Jones, it's probably Dr. Patrick McGovern. As the scientific director at the University of Pennsylvania's Biomolecular Archaeology Laboratory, he not only travels the world uncovering ancient treasures, he uses science to re-create the drinks those ancient people got tipsy on. By performing chemical analysis on the various potshards and containers that the expeditions find buried, "Dr. Pat," as he's known to friends and fans, brings extinct alcoholic beverages back to life after thousands of years. In one of his most impressive feats of Jurassic Park–ing a cold one, he even helped re-create a drink based on 2,700-year-old artifacts found in King Midas's tomb, a honeyed nectar marketed as "Midas Touch." Which, in and of itself, was a pretty compelling reason to get in touch. But when I found out that he'd collaborated with Sam Calagione at the Delaware-based Dogfish Head Brewery to re-create a form of Incan corn beer as well, my curiosity was piqued. And when I learned that this *chicha* beer was actually created using a pre-Columbian method of chewing the corn so that salivary enzymes would turn the starches into sugar . . . well, let's just say I had to learn more. After all, how often do you see brewers chewing up and spitting out their grain before firing up the kettles?

Unfortunately, I was a little late to the party. The Chicha is only released in very limited quantities at the Dogfish Head brewpub and was not on tap at the time of my inquest (although I did find out that Dr. Pat's Chateau Jiahu collaboration with the brewery, based on an ancient Chinese recipe, might be in stock and paired wonderfully with most Asian cuisine). But it wasn't all for naught. I learned from Dr. Pat that indigenous beer was not unique to the Andes; Native Americans used fermentable sugars and wild yeasts to create a wide variety of beverages in many different places, including the modern-day American Southwest. *Maíz,* saguaro sap, perhaps even cacao would have all figured in the drinking habits of the first Americans to inhabit the area. An intriguing prospect for a regional beer historian, to say the least.

And the reason I currently find myself at the Arizona Wilderness Brewing Co., in a strip mall on the outskirts of Phoenix on a one-hundred-and-three-degree day. My brother, who lives in Phoenix, had first told me about the brand back when it was ranked number one among new breweries in 2013 by RateBeer.com. And now, at last, I had a reason to come to Arizona and give it a try. Well, fine, my wife, who is not American, also wanted to see the Grand Canyon. But as any beer lover can attest, it's never a bad idea to sneak a little beer tasting into the itinerary. And while the expert brewers at the Arizona Wilderness Brewing Co. might not have any indigenous southwestern corn *chicha* on the menu for me to try, they do manage to accomplish some pretty amazing things with local ingredients—ingredients that very easily could have figured into Native American brews as well. In the past, they have offered beers made with everything from Sonoran white berries—a nearly extinct native grain used by Apaches in the Chiricahua Mountains—to a black IPA dry-hopped with juniper berries from the Juniper Mesa Wilderness. They've even gone so far as to brew with wild yeasts collected at 9,000 feet, in the mountains north of Flagstaff.

Today, however, it's a session IPA that features mesquite

pods picked from trees directly behind the brewery—no, it doesn't get much more local than that. And if there's anything more refreshing than the air-conditioning pouring in through the vents on this hot Arizona afternoon, it's this beer. It is nothing short of delicious, full of floral notes, with just a slight citrusy tang. As to whether the mesquite pods are the secret ingredient in this magical concoction, I can't really say, but it's tasty regardless—and beats shopping for decorative Kokopelli garden motifs, even with my wife. The perfect combination, I would surmise, between indigenous ingredients and European brewing techniques, coexisting on the cusp of—just as the name suggests—the Arizona wilderness.

Innovative beers like this show the two distinct brewing traditions that came to exist alongside each other in the western United States. Now, I'm not saying Geronimo would have been sipping mesquite pod IPAs while some rough approximation of a hipster asked him if he'd like a second order of green chili pulled-pork sliders. But the brewing of alcoholic beverages did play an indispensable role to many of the Native American and European American inhabitants who came to call the western portions of the United States home. The former utilized it in their most sacred and life-affirming ceremonies, and the latter, as a cornerstone of a saloon culture that would come to define the western experience.

Two distinct legacies of regional American beer, alive and well and definitely commingling in a sunbaked strip mall on the outskirts of Phoenix. Not a bad way to start a chapter—or a hot summer day—in the heart of what still very much feels like America's western frontier. Past the parking lots, the saguaros are undulating drowsily in the heat waves; to the east, the Superstition Mountains are catching the full brunt of the sun; and according to the message I just received, my wife will be looking at Kokopellis for another whole hour yet.

So, yes, I think I will have that second round of green chili pulled-pork sliders, thank you very much. And another one of these good mesquite pod beers while you're at it, pardner.

One of the greatest myths perpetuated by Eurocentric history textbooks is that Native American civilizations did not possess the knowledge or technology to produce alcohol. We're told that intoxicating beverages were introduced by the more "civilized" Europeans who strode in doffing their caps and toasting with fine wines. But this is categorically untrue. The panoply of alcoholic beverages consumed by indigenous Americans prior to the arrival of Columbus is frankly mind-blowing. In fact, one of ol' Christopher's first observations upon arriving in coastal Venezuela was the fact that the inhabitants drank two distinct alcoholic beverages, one from *maíz,* and another from maguey. True, they did not *distill* alcohol, just as Europeans did not before the Middle Ages. And alcoholic beverages did generally play less of a role in parts of North America where tobacco and hallucinogenic plants were the intoxicants of choice. But expert brewers and vintners were to be found in the Americas prior to the arrival of Europeans, alongside sprawling indigenous cities that dwarfed almost anything in Europe, and vast Native American empires that rivaled even Rome.[*]

The Mayans had their *balché,* a drink brewed from tree bark and wild honey. The Indians of what is now British Guiana preferred *paiwari,* a beer made from chewed cassava. The Jíbaros of Ecuador consumed a manioc beer to cel-

---

[*]In terms of pure physical size, the Incan Empire was by far the largest. At its height, it stretched some 2,400 miles from north to south, for a total area of almost 300,000 square miles. Some estimates put as many as twelve million people living within its borders. And yes, they drank lots of beer.

ebrate when the head of an enemy was taken in combat, a sacred yucca beer fermented in earthenware jugs, *and* a sweet wine produced from the fruit of the *chonta* palm—a robust drink list, to say the least. The Matacos, Chorotis, and Ashluslay all made *algoroba* beer, and across Mexico, Nahuatl-speaking people enjoyed then, just as they do today, the delights of *pulque,* a fermented drink made from the agave plant. The inhabitants of Guatemala's Pacific coast even savored, much to the surprise of early Spanish explorers, a drink made from cacao pods, "an abundant liquor of the smoothest taste, between sour and sweet, which is of the most refreshing coolness." Evidently, long before Europeans "discovered" chocolate and turned it into candy bars, Native Americans had already perfected a delicious chocolate liqueur. And that's just the beginning—the list of indigenous beverages goes on and on, including everything from the maple drinks of the Iroquois, to the persimmon wines of the Cherokee. Hog plums, custard apples, pineapples, cashews, wild grapes, sweet potatoes, wild bananas, elderberries, pepper trees, and yes, even mesquite pods . . . if it had starch or sugar in it, someone, somewhere, probably fermented it.

But if there was one drink that stood above all—one that was consumed from the southern peaks of the Andes, straight up to the edge of the Great Plains—it was corn beer. The very *chicha* that Dr. Pat re-created using an ancient recipe for Dogfish Head's Ancient Ales series, and that is still made using traditional methods by many modern-day indigenous peoples. Corn was truly *the* native grain, first domesticated from the wild *teosinte* plant in Mexico's Balsa River Valley around seven or eight thousand years ago. Some archaeological theories suggest that it was actually a thirst for a corn-based wine made from *maíz* stalks that helped propagate the plant beyond its native region. Either way, whether it was for

Native Americans were expert brewers of a vast assortment of intoxicating beverages and incorporated them into many of their most sacred ceremonies. Some beverages had hallucinogenic and, in a few instances, even emetic properties.

corn drinks or corn meal, by 1500 B.C., corn-based agriculture had spread well beyond Mesoamerica. At some point, when corn had become just domesticated enough to produce soft, chewable kernels, corn beer came into the picture. The process of mastication didn't just crush the kernels; it added salivary enzymes that began the process of converting starches into sugar. Essentially, it was an alternative to malting—a way of making a starchy staple more palatable to wild yeasts. And after what was no doubt a considerable amount of chewing and spitting, the first beer in America was born.

The process of making and drinking corn beer was generally ritualized and carefully controlled in most indigenous societies. In an interesting analog to the English alewife, women did much of the brewing. According to early Spanish observers, the Incan rulers of Peru selected a group of beautiful girls to be *mamakona*—essentially beer nuns—who remained chaste and brewed exclusively for the palace. Chewing the corn before spitting it into a collection vessel was a sacred activity to be accompanied by songs and incantations. Once fermented, consumption of the beer was equally regimented. Among the Incas, it was customary for the king to pour *chicha* into a golden bowl, part of "the navel of the universe," as a way of slaking the Sun God's thirst. They even rubbed corn beer on sacrificial victims and force-fed them through tubes while they were buried alive in ceremonial tombs to intoxicate them for the big event. And the most notorious human sacrificers of all, the Aztecs of central Mexico, were equally fond of *chicha* and also incorporated it into their rituals. In some cases, a bit *too* fond, as draconian rules were put into place to control the usage of the intoxicant. With a powerful drink known as the "bone breaker" made from toasted corn, stalk juice, and pepper tree seeds, ready to knock anyone who consumed it right off their feet, it isn't terribly hard to imagine why. To combat wanton intoxication, the Aztec *Codex Ixtlilxochitl* recommended the following rather severe punishments for inebriation outside of the temple:

> Thus the drunkard, if he was plebian, had his hair cut publicly in the market square, and his house was sacked and torn down, because the law said that he who deprived himself of his good judgment was not worthy to have a house but could live in the fields like an animal; and the second time he was punished with death; and if he was noble the first time that he was caught committing this crime he was punished with death.

"Heavily regulated," however, does not necessarily mean "consumed in moderation." Corn beer, and other intoxicants, served a religious purpose: they were a source of visions and altered states, and a means of direct communion with the gods. And when ceremonies mandated, alcohol was consumed in *massive* quantities. The rain dance tradition of the Tohono O'odham people of the Sonoran Desert demonstrates how sacred rituals and overindulgence could go hand in hand. "Much liquor we made," one woman of the tribe remembered, "and we drank it to pull down the clouds." Upon burying the beverages for fermentation, women would chant, "Do you ferment and let us get beautifully drunk." Once that fermentation was complete, it was considered customary to drink a neighbor's alcohol until vomiting ensued, and then to continue drinking at a different neighbor's house after that. It was nothing short of a sacred duty, and a means of strengthening the community and ensuring a bountiful harvest.[*] Such bouts of overindulgence were periodic, though, conducted as part of a larger ceremonial calendar—drunkenness was not a part of everyday life, and a host of taboos and regulations existed to protect celebrants and make sure it did not become one.

Corn beer also traveled north from Mexico, into what today is considered the Southwest and western portions of the United States. It wasn't the only alcoholic beverage consumed—a form of *pulque* called "tulpi" was drunk by some southwestern groups, a saguaro wine was preferred by the Maricopa and Pima of the Sonora, and in California, various tribes were recorded as making a strong cider from manzanita berries. But corn beer, or *tiswin*, as it was known to the

---

[*]And, incidentally, a reason the introduction of distilled spirits by Europeans would prove so destructive to many indigenous cultures later on. To peoples who overindulged on low-alcohol beverages on rare and sacred occasions, the sudden arrival of high-proof spirits, when coupled with a cultural breakdown in sacred traditions, often did have harmful effects.

Chicha, a type of indigenous corn beer, was consumed in many parts of North and South America. Ritual drinking cups like this one were used throughout the Incan Empire.

Apache, was the predominant beverage in what would become Arizona and New Mexico. Unlike older forms of corn beer, *tiswin* was made from sprouted corn that had been dried and ground—that is to say, malted. Beyond that, recipes varied wildly according to tribal and regional preferences. Various ingredients were added to the frothy, pale-colored corn beer, to accentuate its natural sweetness and to enhance its effects, and fasting often took place before it was consumed so that the alcohol would pack more of a punch. *Tiswin* on its own was not very high in alcohol, and as one Apache would later remember,

"It was not much stronger than water—took a lot to make you drunk." The Natty Light of the ancient world, you might even say. But it was popular, and when available, Apaches did consume it in ample quantities, because it was not very difficult to make. An Apache woman named Dahteste, who was with Geronimo in the rebellion days of 1886, shared her recipe:

> To make tiswin you grind corn fine on metate. Build a big fire, boil meal twenty minutes. Take it out, squeeze mash out good. Throw grounds away. Put in jar and let ferment with yeast twenty-four hours. It took much longer when we had no yeast.

In fact, it was *tiswin* that was largely responsible for Geronimo's decision to leave the reservation and return to the traditional lands of his people—on the reservation, Apaches were prohibited by the occupying U.S. military from brewing their sacred drink, or using it in traditional ceremonies. This ban was one insult among many that would eventually lead Geronimo and his followers into open rebellion against an uninvited and alien government. To men like Geronimo—and to many indigenous peoples across North and South America— native alcoholic beverages were not simply a refreshing drink or a welcome intoxicant. They were an essential part of their sacred cosmology, and one of the few direct conduits to the spiritual world. Whether it was called *chicha, tiswin, pulque,* or *tulpi,* such drinks were treated with ceremony, decorum, and great respect. And far from going extinct or being confined to a reservation, indigenous drinks and their distilled progeny continue to be consumed across the Americas to this day, both in their original forms, and in slightly altered states. When the indigenous ingredients met the European technique of distillation, entirely new forms of alcohol were created, drinks with distinctly American identities and flavor profiles that cut across cultural boundaries. After all, bourbon whiskey is little more than distilled corn beer that's been aged in a barrel, and tequila, in all its tangy splendor, is simply a form of *pulque* that's been passed through a still. An interesting note to end on, that two of our most popular and beloved spirits are the direct offspring of the fermented drinks of the very first Americans, and a natural segue into the arrival of European-style beverages to the western frontier.

The concept of "the West" in America has never been static. To colonial Anglo-Americans on the Eastern Seaboard, it constituted the edge of the Appalachian Mountains. In the first decades of America's independence, it came to mean the lands that lay just beyond them. Beginning with the expedition of Lewis and Clark in 1804, and continuing throughout the nineteenth century, though, the West increasingly came to mean the territories that could be found beyond the Mississippi. And with Manifest Destiny all the rage, and Americans convinced that a nation spanning two oceans was within their reach, settling those lands and subjugating their native inhabitants became a top and rather tragic priority. They weren't the first colonizers to settle in the West—the French territory of Louisiana had theoretically included most of the Great Plains, and thanks to early forays made by the Spanish, most of California and the Southwest were nominally part of Mexico. The colonial presence in the western half of North America had been relatively weak, though, with the French and Spanish focusing most of their attention on the more profitable plantation colonies of the Caribbean and Latin America. This part of the continent that was unknown to most Europeans was a tempting prospect for immigrants

In the Southwest, elements of both European and Native American brewing often coexisted in close proximity. In this photo, a saloon in Arizona displays indigenous motifs.

who had come to America searching for what they could not find at home: a piece of land to call their own. Just as Scots-Irish pioneers had escaped the seaboard to homestead the Appalachian wilderness, and just as German Americans had left New York and Philadelphia to set up shop in the Middle West, a fresh batch of hopeful Americans from a wide variety of backgrounds began packing their bags and loading up the covered wagons in the middle years of the nineteenth century.

And they brought plenty of alcohol with them, although for the very first settlers, this seldom meant beer. Going west entailed carrying whiskey—it was an essential, practically a form of currency in a place where paper money didn't do anyone much good. Even the Lewis and Clark expedition had brought six kegs of the hard stuff with them, only to run out by Great Falls. In part, this preference for whiskey was shaped by the same geographic factors that made it prevalent in the mountain South: it was nonperishable and easily transportable in a region with few roads and widely dispersed settlements. But there were economic considerations as well. Whiskey not only appreciated in value the more time it spent in the barrel—its value also increased exponentially the farther away it was sold from eastern civilization. In the 1830s, a barrel of low-quality whiskey could be purchased in St. Louis for as little as 25 cents. By the time it reached Fort Leavenworth in Kansas, that same barrel might sell for 34 dollars, and by Yellowstone, well, a business-savvy settler could value that cheap barrel of whiskey at as much as 64 dollars. The whiskey could then be traded for much-needed supplies, used to procure the assistance of an experienced guide, or, as was often the case, simply kept for personal use. Not surprisingly, because of the high values placed on early frontier whiskey, the quality plummeted. Whiskey peddlers sold watered-down and adulterated "barrel whiskey" to pioneers, and oftentimes an even fouler concoction to Native Americans, who had little experience with stronger spirits and were exploited in the cruelest of ways. The initial crop of western saloons that sprang up at dusty frontier outposts were crude, whiskey-selling establishments—forget refrigeration and carbonation. With wagon trains and stagecoaches taking months to cross the plains, getting a bulky barrel of beer to the West was at best impractical and, at worst, flat-out impossible. Whiskey was the obvious choice.

Until the train came along, that is. The same technological innovations that had allowed the dizzying growth of midwestern breweries in the second half of the nineteenth century also brought beer to America's westernmost outposts. By 1869, the first transcontinental railroad had already spanned the coasts and made western rail shipping possible. And refrigerated railcars changed the game entirely. When coupled with regional icehouses, not to mention the more shelf-stable pasteurized bottles that would come later, beer became an everyday commodity. By 1876, grocers and saloons in Denver, Colorado, were already advertising Anheuser-Busch's "St. Louis Lager Beer." By 1884, the company had thirteen agencies in Texas alone, all storing, cooling, and distributing Budweiser beer for the thirsty inhabitants of the Lone Star State. The competing St. Louis firm of William J. Lemp had branch offices in such far-flung cities as Leadville, El Paso, Wichita, and even Salt Lake City. And when the Jos. Schlitz Brewing Co. brought suit against the Southern Pacific Railway regarding what they saw as unreasonable shipping rates and unfair practices, many of the more powerful brewers decided to forgo the crooked rail barons entirely and began buying trains of their own. Anheuser-Busch played a significant part in the establishment of the Manufacturers Railway Company, and Joseph Uihlein, a major figure in Schlitz management, was the true owner of the Union Refrigerator Transit Corporation. With time, the gargantuan breweries of America's heartland made significant inroads into its westernmost fringes.

But not all westerners were content to wait around on the next beer shipment, or to be totally reliant on brewers back east. Indeed, small local breweries had been making beer since before the railroads. And even after they came along, railways didn't extend to every western town, and packaged beer didn't always survive the long journey in peak condition. One very early example of regional western brewing comes courtesy of the first German settlers of San Antonio, who arrived in Texas in 1844 under the leadership of Carl Prince of Solms-Braunfels, just prior to annexation. Back in Germany, or even back east, for that matter, a weary farmer could retire "after his evening meal and a glass of beer or wine, [and] go upstairs

According to the billboard, railroads and Pabst beer were two of the nation's greatest achievements. That may be debatable, but the former did bring the latter to the American West.

to his room and stretch his tired limbs on a bed, even though it be only a mattress of straw." In Texas, though, Prince Carl noted, "there is no strengthening drink of beer or wine on the table whereby he could refresh himself." Even after beer did finally arrive on the scene, it was anything but accessible. He would write to prospective newcomers to his little German colony: "The only thing that is really expensive is wine, beer, and any kind of alcoholic drinks. The beer is imported from the United States, and is very strong. One called this kind of beer ale. I do not think it can be kept in good condition during summer." Evidently, these early Texans not only had to put up with outrageous prices, but extra-strong import-grade ale from the East, a far cry from the cool, crisp lagers they preferred.

Such hardships, though, were not to last. Prince Carl even-

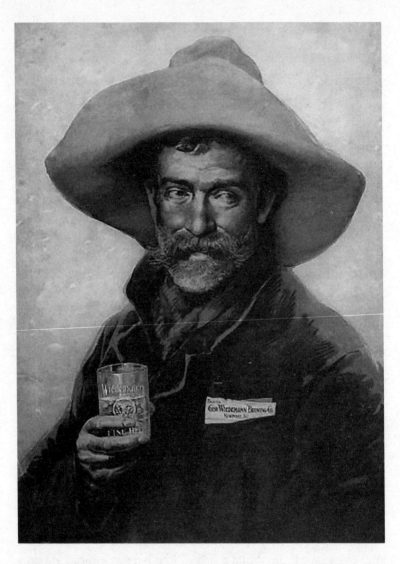

Although whiskey kept better in frontier conditions, beer wasn't far behind once a new western settlement became established. Trains brought both beer and ice to thirsty cowboys and miners.

tually hung up his cowboy hat and returned to Germany, but many of his fellow settlers stayed. And by 1855, a delicious lager beer—or at the very least, a lager yeast beer, if it was not cold-conditioned—was being produced by a brewer and cooper named William A. Menger. His brewery was so successful, he also built a hotel to accommodate drunken visitors, and he began delivering his stock all across the state in wagons and oxcarts. Menger would pave the way for Lone Star beer, originally brewed by the Alamo Brewing Company of San Antonio in 1874 and later acquired by Anheuser-Busch, not to mention the Spoetzl Brewery, founded near the town of Shiner in 1909. The latter produced then, just as it does today, a Shiner bock beer—a darker, maltier style of Bavarian lager that was largely eclipsed by paler lagers in the late nineteenth and early twentieth centuries. Both Lone Star and Shiner are still beloved by Texans, something akin to the "national" beers of a people who have never forgotten—nor miss a chance to remind you—that the Lone Star State was once, however briefly, an independent republic.

Texas led the pack when it came to western brewing, but other territories were quick to catch up. When silver was discovered in Nevada, breweries weren't far behind the prospectors—at least twenty-one breweries could be found in the territory by 1871, scattered across towns like Eureka and Carson City. In the supposedly abstemious Mormon lands of Utah, eager settlers not only produced a crude whiskey called "Valley Tan," but also beer. By 1884, the territory of Utah could claim some eighteen breweries to its name, with three in Salt Lake City alone. The Idaho Territory had four breweries to wash down its spuds, the Montana Territory had no fewer than three breweries in Virginia City and four in Helena, and Arizona, although it lagged behind its competition, did make gains once malt was made available from San Francisco via the railroads. So much so, that in 1885, the city of Phoenix was actually able to make an entire sidewalk with discarded beer bottles. The streets of the frontier town may not have been paved with gold, as many eager migrants had hoped, but they were paved with beer.

Even Judge Roy Bean's joint advertised "Ice Beer" to parched Texans. This photograph shows a horse thief being tried on the front porch of the saloon.

Breweries sprang up in large numbers across the western frontier, but the progress the beer industry made in the deserts and plains would be dwarfed by the rise of mountain brewing in Colorado, and with good reason: the high elevations meant lower temperatures and an ample supply of ice, both of which made lager brewing considerably easier at a time when refrigeration was either expensive or lacking altogether. The Gold Rush of 1857 and 1858 brought wagonloads of miners into Colorado, and just as in other territories, beer came along for the ride. In fact, a large brewery was up and running in the town of Auraria in just one year. It was an early attempt at mountain brewing, and some ingredients weren't easy to come by—one drinker remembered that "though quite drinkable, [it] was as innocent of hops as our early whiskey was of wheat or old rye"—but it was a start. By 1861, a larger, more professional establishment called the Tivoli Brewing Co. was already brewing bock beer in Denver, and the towns of Laporte and Boulder had sizable breweries by 1862 and 1875, respectively.

Then Adolph Coors came to town. Born in Germany, like many western brewers, Adolph had been a brewer's apprentice in Dortmund and later worked at breweries in Berlin and Kassel. After coming to America, he hopscotched around the German neighborhoods of New York and Chicago, only to discover that both the East and the Midwest were already saturated with German American breweries. The West, on the other hand, was still wide open and considered fair game. So in 1872, he relocated to Denver and established a bottling business, which proved to be a nice stepping-stone to opening his own brewery the very next year, in a town called Golden, just a few miles outside of Denver. Using a pilsner-style beer recipe purchased from a Czech immigrant, he and his partner, Jacob Schueler, began making their crisp, pale lager. By the 1880s, their brewery was already one of the largest and best equipped of the twenty-three breweries in the Rocky Mountains. Just like that, the high-altitude ancestor of "the Silver Bullet" was born—destined to produce one of the most popular beers in the American West, and to one day become the largest single brewery facility in the world.

The advent of canned beer and home refrigeration would one day turn beer drinking into a domestic activity—but those days were still a long ways away on the western frontier of the late nineteenth century. The hardscrabble assortment of cowboys, ranchers, farmers, and miners drank beer not in the home, but in the saloon. Just as the English-style tavern had become the center of town life in New England, and the German-derived beer garden a mainstay of midwestern culture, the western saloon managed to serve as town hall, political society, gambling parlor, dance hall, courthouse, and social club, all at the same time. As a saloon was oftentimes one of the few reliably populated public structures in a western town, it was only natural that much of the settlement's social life would occur inside its batwing doors. Kentucky bourbon, which the railroads had made available west of the Mississippi, was always a favorite, as were an elaborate array of western cocktails.* But the combined supplies of local brews and imported labels from the East meant that once a town and a railroad were both firmly established, there were usually buckets of beer to be had by all. At the infamous Long Branch Saloon in Dodge City, Anheuser-Busch was on tap, kept cold in the summer by ice shipped in from the mountains of Colorado. A saloon owned by George Brown in Big Spring, Texas, only served beer, with customers using kegs as stools and drawing nickel drafts from ice-cold barrels. When natural ice wasn't available, beer was often kept cool in nearby streams, or simply served at room temperature—at least, until artificial refrigeration came into the picture. In most cases, the saloon was one of the few places a tired westerner could relax among friends, and sometimes enjoy a cold drink.

The saloon may have been heralded as a great achievement by the thirsty cowhands, ranchers, and miners who flocked to enjoy the liquid comforts of its polished bar, but it gained its fair share of detractors as well. Between 1850 and 1890, the population of the United States increased fourfold; its

---

* It's not something you see much in cowboy movies, but cocktails were standard fare in western saloons. In addition to beer and whiskey, thirsty gunslingers enjoyed sherry cobblers, gin and bitters, spiced wines, and a host of other mixed drinks one wouldn't normally associate with High Noon. Oh, and oysters—pickled or canned, they were popular in western saloons, too.

consumption of beer, however, grew twenty-four-fold, from 36 million gallons to 855 million gallons. Saloons also grew in number, from some 100,000 in 1870, to 300,000 by 1900. And it doesn't take a genius to tell that the two numbers were related, and closely at that. Some of the beer did simply replace whiskey, a beverage that had fallen comparatively out of favor due to the meteoric rise of German lager. But the explosion of immigrant-owned breweries had spurred a dramatic upsurge in immigrant-owned saloons as well. And while saloons were prevalent in the immigrant neighborhoods of eastern cities like New York and Boston, the relative isolation of western towns and the skewed ratios of rowdy young men to women certainly made the western saloon among the most visible—and notorious. In Leadville, South Dakota, a town with a population of 20,000, there was one saloon for every 100 inhabitants—women and children included—and similar ratios were to be found in towns across the West. Some of these establishments were no doubt pleasant, clean, and upstanding places. But just as many were replete with "the stench of stale beer and whiskey often mixed with the nauseating smell of vomit on the sidewalks," as one visitor to a western town noticed. And it was certainly no secret that the bulk of these saloons had direct ties to major German American–owned breweries. After all, men like Gustave Pabst and Adolphus Busch had spent a fortune bankrolling saloons across the West and plastering then with every Custer painting and branded piece of schwag they could come up with. German names like theirs were everywhere. Then, of course, there were also all those gunfights and beer brawls.

To many Americans—particularly those of British Protestant backgrounds and nativist leanings—the stability of their country seemed to be under threat, thanks to a rising tide of ethnic newcomers. Of course, this was total hogwash.

The idea of an original "American" people was flawed from the start. As even a cursory study of American history (or a scan of the first few chapters of this book) would have shown, the country had been a diverse melting pot from the get-go: a place where Dutchmen and Dominicans could trade rounds on the streets of New Amsterdam, English aristocrats might pick up techniques to make molasses beers from more experienced West Africans, and Scots-Irish settlers could master a new whiskey grain with a little help from the Cherokee. Hardly the homogenous land of teetotalers that the emerging temperance movement imagined. But the privileged economic role many Anglo-Americans had enjoyed began to feel precarious, and "foreign" elements made a convenient scapegoat. By the first decade of the twentieth century, native-born Americans were increasingly demanding a national ban on the saloons and the drinks that they served. Drunkenness was seen as a scourge brought by immigrants, rather than the reality of American life it had always been—the Pilgrims, after all, were not drinking Kool-Aid, and George Washington was hardly one to toast with Tang.

The temperance movement didn't begin in the West—Maine had been at the vanguard of an earlier prohibition push that banned alcohol completely in the state in 1851, and Chicago had even experienced a "lager beer riot" in 1855, when German and Irish immigrants reacted violently to a series of new antisaloon legislation. But the unique circumstances and emerging regional politics of the West certainly added a tremendous dose of fuel to the flames and brought local antialcohol legislation at the state and county level long before it became the law of the land. The Progressive movement of the late nineteenth and early twentieth centuries took on a life of its own west of the Mississippi, and while its aims were both high and admirable, it had a darker side as well. Yes, it did promote equality and women's suffrage—a number of western states had given women the vote well before the 1920 passage of the Nineteenth Amendment. But it also gave birth to the hatchet-swinging harridan known as Carrie Nation, whose respect for private property stopped at the very saloon doors she hacked to pieces. It did increase the regulation of mining, railroad, and ranching interests that were growing wildly out of control, in a part of the country where government oversight had been weak. Yet it also allowed populist hate groups like the Ku Klux Klan to control local governments across the Rockies and the Northwest. Reform was all the rage, but increasingly, it came to mean driving out all that was deemed foreign and un-American in the name of bettering this new, "progressive" society.

Unfortunately for America, alcohol was to take the brunt of the blow. Suffragettes, Klansmen, Progressives, and Populists from around the country may not have agreed on much, but for once, they all seemed to find common ground in their dislike of drinking and drinking establishments. With the spoken aim of protecting the American family, and the unspoken goal of disempowering immigrants and Catholics, for whom saloons and the production of alcohol were often cultural staples, the crusade against booze began, under the leadership of the Anti-Saloon League. As an ominous precursor to what was to come, Congress passed the Sixteenth Amendment in 1916, establishing a national income tax to make up for the loss of government alcohol revenues that were not far in the offing. The next year, when the 65th Congress convened, "dries" already outnumbered "wets" by 140 to 64 in the Democratic Party, and 138 to 62 in the Republican Party. And with the declaration of war against Germany that April, the formerly vociferous heads of German American breweries suddenly found it best to keep their mouths shut—anti-

It was somewhat ironic that the American West—a region where life centered on the saloon—also produced many of Prohibition's earliest champions. Even before the Volstead Act went into effect, most western states were already dry.

German sentiment had reached a fevered pitch, and zealots like Wayne Wheeler of the Anti-Saloon League were actively calling out the "alien enemies" who controlled such household names as Pabst and Anheuser-Busch. When the Eighteenth Amendment was finally ratified, and Prohibition became official, it almost felt redundant, especially in the West, where most states had already been dry for several years. On January 16, 1920, the Volstead Act went into effect, and across the country, an industry that had helped nourish a nation and power a people for nearly three centuries ground to a halt. The unthinkable had occurred: beer was, to the dismay of its brewers and much of the public, completely verboten.

But wouldn't you know—people didn't stop drinking. Not by a *long* shot. The mild-mannered, law-abiding, churchgoing era that the Anti-Saloon League and its promoters envisioned turned out to be fantasy, and the "noble experiment" proved to have some rather ignoble results. Bootlegging flourished, organized crime took control of the wheel, and in the speakeasies and blind tigers that sprang up all over America, the Jazz Age was born. Culturally, America was flourishing, as writers like F. Scott Fitzgerald, musicians like Louis Armstrong, and singers like Ella Fitzgerald combined their voices to make the 1920s roar. And the country's drinking habits were more scandalous and decadent than ever, as a young generation of Americans came to realize they didn't want to sip a thimble-full of Grandma's blackberry cordial—they wanted to get *loaded*.

And so they did, with the drinking culture of the day aimed at the ultimate goal of inebriation. The government had deemed alcohol a powerful intoxicant rather than something to be savored, and the nation's youth took that to heart. Cocktails became standard fare in urban speakeasies for the same reason they had first been popular in western saloons: they helped disguise the taste of cheap, poorly made spirits. And poorly made, these spirits were. People mostly drank bathtub gin and low-grade moonshine whiskey, with illicit rum from the Caribbean and blended scotch from Canada available for those who could pay. In either case, the spirits were contraband, which meant that low volume and high potency were

With the arrival of Prohibition, American drinking habits literally changed overnight. What had been a cultural staple suddenly became a controlled substance. In this photograph, 749 cases of illegal beer are being destroyed.

key. It was far easier to smuggle a bottle of spirits across state lines than a keg of beer, and that bottle of spirits could stay on the speakeasy shelf almost indefinitely. Beer was simply too bulky, too low in alcohol, and too hard to mix with anything else. For people who just wanted to get hammered on the sly, a rich, thirst-quenching, high-volume product made no sense. The drinkers of America turned their attention away from their beer steins and became besotted instead with a martini glass of the hard stuff.

But beer lovers are a notoriously stubborn—and nostalgic—lot. And there were more than a few who weren't going to go down without a fight. Some smaller breweries were able to stay under the radar; Al Capone controlled no fewer than six breweries in the Chicago area alone, all of which continued to produce beer in the shadow of the Volstead Act. Larger, more prominent breweries couldn't risk flouting the rules so publicly, but they did offer a range of suspicious malted syrups that, although ostensibly used for baking, could quite easily be put into service by a resourceful home brewer. And then there was the infamous "needle beer." As breweries struggled to stay afloat, many continued to brew nonalcoholic beer for the general public. And it didn't take the general public long to figure out that just a squirt of grain alcohol from a syringe could turn a mug of legal nonalcoholic beer into something that had at least a passing resemblance to the full-bodied brews they had known from before. Unfortunately, the resemblance was precisely that: passing. Although initial sales of nonalcoholic beers marketed under names like Bevo and Manna looked promising—300,000,000 gallons were produced in 1921 alone—the enthusiasm didn't last. By 1932, that number had dropped to 85,000,000 gallons, as America's boozehounds came around to the fact that they'd rather drink real moonshine than fake beer. But the production of such nonalcoholic beers did offer at least some source of income to the country's harried brewers.

In most cases, though, malted syrups and needle beer were not enough to keep a brewery in business. Prohibition was a disaster for the American brewing industry, wreaking havoc in a way unseen before or since. Leaders like New York's Jacob Ruppert used their positions in the USBA to lobby on the industry's behalf, pleading with the government to allow the production of low-alcohol "near beer" at the very least. But their protests were in vain, and breweries had to find creative ways to keep from going under. Some, like Anheuser-Busch and Yuengling, capitalized on their existing fleet of refrigerated trucks to sell ice cream. Schlitz, Miller, and Pabst turned their attention to cheese, chocolate, and other confections. And soft drinks were produced on a scale that would change America's palate forever, with ginger ale and root beer being made by chagrined brewmasters, to supply the soda fountains that had replaced taverns as social centers. Some resorted to fruit juices, breakfast cereals, and yeast extracts, others to animal feed, vinegar, and industrial alcohol—desperate breweries were willing to try just about anything.

In the West, however, one brewery in particular would emerge looking golden: Coors. Adolph, the founding father of the venture, along with his sons Adolph Jr., Herman, and Grover, had possessed the foresight to diversify the business well before the Volstead Act effectively shut down their beer-making capacity. The manufacturing wing of his company devoted itself to porcelain—a version of which still exists today—while the construction wing dealt in cement and real estate during an era in which construction was booming across the West. Its brewing facilities, meanwhile, focused on the sale of malted milk—much of it going to the Mars candy company, to be used in the variety of chocolate bars that were replacing cold beers as the standard after-work treat. When Prohibition finally ended, when the din subsided and the smoke cleared, the handful of large, resourceful breweries like Coors that had managed to weather the thirteen-year storm were virtually all that remained of the nation's beer makers. The stage was set and the market was ready: the age of the American macrobrew was about to begin.

I t's easy to poke fun at the mass-produced American beer labels that have formed the bulk of our nation's brewing industry for very nearly a century—they're an easy target. And while even the snootiest of beer connoisseurs may still enjoy a macrobrew nostalgically at a ball game or ironically at a dive bar, it's no great secret that many contemporary drinkers turn up their noses at the same quotidian can of suds their parents and grandparents savored. Perhaps with good reason.

To survive Prohibition, breweries with the resources often switched to making nonalcoholic products. This advertisement extols the virtues of Coors Malted Milk. The smaller breweries that could not adapt generally went under.

After all, compared to the darker, richer, more character-driven beers that existed in America before Prohibition, and when put alongside the traditional European ales and lagers that never went out of style in the first place, the American macrobrew can indeed be a disappointment. The malt is generally weak and one-dimensional, the hops are usually bland and lacking in aromatics, and the drinker is often left feeling overcarbonated and underwhelmed. But before we judge such beers too harshly, we should consider where they came from in the first place. The pale lager of the twentieth century was born directly out of calamity and desperation, and all of us—brewers, consumers, and everyday citizens—helped bring it into existence. We as a nation collectively made it so.

Prohibition was finally repealed in 1933, not because of an intellectual epiphany or cultural awakening, but because of the greatest economic disaster America had ever faced. In the wake of the stock market crash of 1929, the country's economy was in free fall—the Great Depression had begun, and suddenly the United States Treasury was desperate for cash. In the past, taxes on alcohol had supplied the federal government with up to 40 percent of its revenue, and with banks closing and stocks plummeting, it finally occurred to the bright minds in Washington that perhaps shutting down the brewing and distilling infrastructure of America had not been such a good idea after all. In just a few short years, they went from hunting down illegal brewmasters and smashing their barrels, to all but begging them to get the brew kettles fired up and working again.

With only one small problem: there were hardly any American breweries left. Of the 1,392 breweries that had existed prior to Prohibition, a measly 164 remained by its end to supply America's beer—a tall order, any way you look at it. And those that did survive the turmoil were for the most part in dire financial straits. Thirteen years without being able to sell beer had taken their toll—the pressing issue wasn't necessarily about a return to the high standards of before, but of simple survival. Keeping the American beer industry alive inevitably meant cutting corners, and many brewers quite understandably did what they could to get back on their feet quickly. All in the midst of the Great Depression, no less, a time when many were struggling to eat, let alone drink.

As for consumers, the years of Prohibition also had a lasting effect. An entire generation of drinkers had come of age at a time when beer was essentially nonexistent, and sugary cocktails and soft drinks were all the rage. Alcohol during the Roaring Twenties wasn't supposed to be well-made or full of complex flavors—it was simply expected to be easy to swallow and to get you drunk. The collective memory of the hoppy, rich, Bavarian-style lagers that had existed before Prohibition was replaced instead by a thirst for anything cold, bubbly, and cloyingly sweet. American tastes had changed. Somewhere down in the glittering world of the speakeasy, we'd learned to drink watered-down cocktails and forgotten how to drink well-made beer.

From these circumstances emerged the American macrobrew: a sweeter, more watery, and less flavorful version of the original American pale lager that had slowly evolved in the decades after the Civil War. With the hobbled breweries struggling to make a profit again, and Americans with stunted taste buds happy to drink a beer that was simply alcoholic, nobody was complaining. To an impoverished industry and a weary public, it was enough to have the beer taps flowing again. Cheaper and more sweet-tasting adjuncts like corn were used in greater proportions than ever, original high-gravity recipes were diluted to stretch the barley supply even further, lagering times were frequently cut in half, and in

President Franklin Roosevelt signing "the Beer Bill" in 1933, effectively bringing Prohibition to a close. Brewers were ecstatic, but they still had considerable work ahead of them to get back on their feet.

some cases, even a hop extract replaced the zesty and complex bouquet of actual hops. Americans across the board wanted a cheap, easy-drinking beer, and that was exactly what we got.

Even so, convincing Americans to become beer drinkers again took time. Prior to 1914, per capita annual consumption had been roughly 21 gallons—a hefty average. By 1933, that number had plunged to less than 9 gallons a year. In the year that followed Prohibition's repeal, just over 20 million barrels were taxed by the federal government—significantly less than the 60 million barrels that had regularly been taxed in the years before the Volstead Act came into effect. Cocktails, soft drinks, and good ol'-fashioned milk all competed with beer. But by cutting production costs, and by capitalizing on advancements in bottling technology—home refrigeration

The same fine beverage

ACME BEER

can be obtained in restaurants, hotels and
stores . . . the first day its sale is legal.
CALIFORNIA BREWING ASSOCIATION
Brewers of Acme Beer
762 Fulton St., San Francisco   Tel. FIllmore 2700
▶ **RETAILERS SHOULD ORDER NOW** ◀

A western beer brand celebrates the end of Prohibition with an advert urging
retailers to put in their new orders. They assure customers it's "the same fine
beverage," although with the Great Depression and World War II looming, it
is a promise that will prove difficult to keep.

was becoming commonplace, and pasteurized bottled beer
generally lasted longer than draught—the recovering breweries were able to make up for lost time. The introduction of
the first canned beer in 1935 by the Krueger Brewing Co. of
Newark further reduced costs and shelf life and improved the
beverage's domestic appeal. Pabst Export Beer followed in its
footsteps, and soon, cheaper canned beer was being adopted
by breweries and drinkers across the land. An article from the
trade publication *Modern Brewery Age* sums it all up quite
nicely:

> Those who prefer to drink their beer in taverns will
> always find that source open to them. But [with] this new
> form of merchandizing—whether it is "canned beer" or

the "stubby bottle"—reaching the low income homes and bringing in its development increased beer consumption . . . should be encouraged in every possible way.

More and more, beer was being drunk in the home, and breweries began focusing their attention on home consumers. Brewers were initially uneasy at the thought of advertising in the years after Prohibition, with a host of local antialcohol regulations still in place and the fear of the ban still fresh in their memories. But that reticence didn't last long, as the obvious benefits of advertising for attracting a new breed of domestic consumer quickly became clear. At a tavern or saloon, a beer drinker's options were limited to whatever the barkeep had on tap—and given the practice of brewery sponsorships, that selection was usually not very robust. At the store, on the other hand, the consumer could take his or her pick from an array of beer brands. All at once, it was of the utmost importance to convince that consumer that one specific brand of beer trumped all the rest—an ironic claim, given that American beer had become more uniform and lacking in individuality than ever. Anything stronger and more distinct was simply unsalable, possessing, as one nostalgic beer drinker would note, "just too much hop for this generation." But alas, such was the expertise of Madison Avenue.

And it worked. It took time, but the measures slowly kicked in. By 1940, sales of beer were roughly what they had been before Prohibition—a feat accomplished with less than half as many breweries. Through rampant consolidation and growth, the industry had become dominated by a handful of brewing powerhouses, most of which are familiar to the American beer drinker today. That same year, Anheuser-Busch, Pabst, Schlitz, Schaefer, Ballantine, and Ruppert were all producing over a million barrels a year, with Anheuser-Busch number one with over two million. And if there were any voices in the indus-

It wasn't easy to convince Americans to start drinking beer again after Prohibition, but by the 1940s, we had become once again a nation of beer lovers.

try suggesting a return to pre-Prohibition lager, with its richer malts and more robust flavors, they were quickly silenced by the outbreak of war. As the United States found itself drawn into the tumult of World War II, the government recognized beer as the inherent morale booster that it was. If Uncle Sam was going to ask G.I.s to dodge bullets and bombs in the farthest corners of the globe, the least he could do was give them a cold one. The nation's brewers saw the opportunity and responded enthusiastically, citing beer's naturally high vitamin B content as an additional incentive. Accordingly, the government bought beer in bulk, requesting 15 percent of total production for servicemen, an order that boosted the industry tremendously, but also cut into the nation's rationed grain supply, as noted by this *New York Times* article from August 1, 1943:

In March the WPB said that malt was needed to make alcohol for munition; that brewers must cut their use of it 7 per cent under the 1942 figures. To make up the deficiency, brewers turned to corn and rice. Now breweries are feeling the pinch of the nation-wide corn shortage . . .

As one might expect, the brewers did what they had to do to fill the orders, upping the adjuncts and diluting the flavor of American beer even further. But who was going to complain? Not a hardworking American public, which was making sacrifices galore to help with the war effort, and certainly not servicemen, who were a long way from home and preparing to make the ultimate sacrifice of them all. *Any* American beer was greatly appreciated, for the taste of home that it truly was, as indicated by this recorded conversation between a commanding officer and a mess sergeant, featured in *Modern Brewery Age*:

COMMANDING OFFICER: *Do I understand that the water you get here is unsafe?*
MESS SERGEANT: *Yes, sir.*
COMMANDING OFFICER: *What precaution do you take to ensure the health of the outfit?*
MESS SERGEANT: *We filter the water first, sir.*
COMMANDING OFFICER: *Yes.*
MESS SERGEANT: *Then we boil it.*
COMMANDING OFFICER: *Yes?*
MESS SERGEANT: *Then we add chemicals to it.*
COMMANDING OFFICER: *Yes.*
MESS SERGEANT: *And, then, sir, we drink beer.*

In helping to save the free world, brewers also saved their own industry. During the war years of the 1940s, production

In World War II, thirsty servicemen helped bring the American beer industry back to life—the government put in huge orders to keep the troops stocked. The injection of capital got breweries going full steam again, but due to grain rationing, the flavor profile of American beer became generally less malty and complex.

of beer grew by over 40 percent, eventually exceeding pre-Prohibition levels. And the demands of greater production in many cases meant expansion to new territory—a problem that large breweries solved by buying out smaller, more distant breweries, or simply by building new regional franchise breweries that produced the same beer.

By the 1950s, though, with the war won and the nation thriving, finding new beer markets increasingly meant going west. Not the mining towns or cattle stops that breweries had alighted upon a century before, but the *far* West: the burgeoning cities and suburbs of California, a state whose population had exploded during and immediately after the war. In 1953, the Theo Hamm Brewing Co. bought out the Rainier brewery in San Francisco. In 1954, Anheuser-Busch built a brewery in Los Angeles for the then unthinkable sum of $20,000,000, while Pabst took over another Los Angeles brewery to make sure its Blue Ribbon beer was available as well. And as for Schlitz, that same year, it built a brand-new plant in Van Nuys, California, that could on its own turn out a million barrels a year. But cans and bottles, mind you, not barrels, were the name of the game. This was the blossoming of the atomic age, a period of suburban homes and automobiles, of microwaves and TV dinners. American consumers didn't want old-timey products and carefully crafted goods—they wanted cheap and convenient, uniform and reliable, shiny and new. And after decades of corporate consolidation and mechanized mass production, the canned beers that sat in our fridges were exactly that. A far cry from the handcrafted Dutch ales, dark English porters, and complex German lagers that our predecessors had enjoyed, but precisely what we, as a people exhausted by all those years of prohibition, depression, and war, were after. We weren't interested in going downtown to some ethnic saloon, to sing old folk songs and sip at a stein of malty lager. We just wanted to finish mowing the lawn, turn on the tube, and crack open a cold one. Progress—or so we thought.

But something must have changed, no? Or how else could it come to pass that here, in the twenty-first century, a man might sit in a suburban strip mall outside of Phoenix, Arizona, enjoying one of the most deliciously complex session IPAs he has ever tasted in his life, with nary a can of macrobrew in sight?

Indeed, something did change, and to find its origins, we'll have to go a bit farther west yet. The big beer conglomerates may have driven most of the traditional California breweries out of business, but a couple of throwbacks just barely managed to slip through the cracks—one of which was destined to change the course of American beer in the most unexpected of ways.

So get ready. That craft beer revolution we've been all been waiting for is about to begin, with its earliest champions to be found not in any venerable eastern city, but rather on our country's westernmost and *grooviest* coast.

(Cue the Beach Boys.)

CHAPTER 6

THE WEST COAST

or

Wish They All Could Be

California Brews

"WHEN ALL ELSE FAILS," ONE OLD BREWING ADAGE GOES, "make a batch of beer." And indeed, from the advancements in medieval urban beer-craft that were made possible by the plague, to the American lagers that came about thanks to foreign revolutions, innovations in brewing have often been born of accidents and calamity. But an earthquake? No, I've never heard of any Richter-related beer. But as Mark Carpenter, the brewmaster at San Francisco's legendary Anchor Brewing Company informs me, such a thing does exist, and it was during the Loma Prieta quake of 1989 that it came into existence. "We had the earthquake, the power shut down, and there were brews in process. Another brewer and I volunteered to spend the night, in case the power came back on. We had candles, we were having some beer, and as it happened, we were the first ones in the area to get the power back."

And what did they do? "We finished the brew," he tells me with a nostalgic and slightly mischievous grin, "although the batch had caramelized a bit from sitting so long. We thought about dumping it, but Fritz, the owner, had the idea of bottling it with an upside-down label." This "Earthquake Beer," as it came to be known, went on to become something of a collector's item, and the distinctive bottles still turn up on eBay and other auction sites from time to time. It was the type of thing that could only happen in California, due in part to fault lines, but even more so to the sort of unexpected innovations that the folks at the Anchor Brewing Company seem to be adept at creating. Indeed, the brewery itself was something of an anomaly, back when Frederick "Fritz" Maytag purchased it in 1965 to save it from closing down. At the time, it was practically the last of its kind, one of the few remnants of an old San Francisco brewing culture that first came on the scene in the mid-nineteenth century, when the town was still a scrappy frontier port, and a local style of lager known as "steam beer" was the only thing on tap. The brewery survived the big quake of 1906 (the company if not the building itself), and if the old-timers in Potrero Hill are to be believed, it even continued to offer clandestine beer for weddings and special occasions right through Prohibition. But the nail in the coffin—it seemed, anyway—was the arrival of the mass-produced brews from places farther east in the middle of the twentieth century. Beer at the time was considered a uniform commodity, a bit like white bread, as Mark Carpenter remembers. It wasn't expected to have any art or craft to it. Or very much flavor, for that matter. Anchor's steam beer was noticeably maltier and hoppier than the watered-down macrobrews, although because of outdated equipment, batch consistency was always an issue, and its reputation suffered as a result. But on the brink of going out of business, the brewery was saved, by a prescient newcomer with a passion for beer. Fritz Maytag purchased the aging facility for next to nothing and worked hard to make it into something modern and respectable—without forsaking its unique San Francisco heritage. One of the first and smartest moves he made, was hiring a young local who happened to wander into the brewery. "I was real lucky," Mark tells me as we leave his office and make our way toward the brew kettles. "I grew up here, and living through the sixties, many people were looking for different kinds of jobs and lifestyles. I wanted that, too. And I was always a beer drinker. In the early '70s, I took a tour, and I thought it would be a good job while I was figuring out what to do with my life. Fritz hired me, and it worked out for both of us."

The location has changed over the years, but the Anchor Brewing Company is still making distinct styles of local beer in the heart of San Francisco. Its famous Anchor Steam Beer has roots that stretch back to the earliest days of the Gold Rush, when ice for lagering was hard to come by, and beer was brewed and stored at warmer temperatures.

More than forty years later, it still appears to be working out quite well. We pass the hop room and take a quick detour through the loading dock, where crates upon crates of packaged beer are stacked and waiting. For sure, there is the original Anchor Steam Beer, but now also Anchor IPA, Anchor Porter, Anchor Summer Wheat, Anchor Saison—all the rich brew styles you'd come to expect from a successful craft brewery. And as it turns out, Anchor Brewing Company isn't just any old craft brewery. It was arguably the *first* craft brewery. And the movement it started in the late '60s and early '70s forever changed brewing in the United States.

Smiling in his spotless white workman's jumpsuit, Mark leads the way and takes me back toward the cool invitation of the taproom, still as passionate about beer as the first day he walked in, still as enamored with the art and the craft of it as a brewer can be. A California original, any way you look at it.

A quick glance at my watch confirms that it's perhaps a *little* early for a beer, but then again, the whole state is in the midst of one of its perennial droughts, and conserving water, as I've been told, is a civic duty.

So a cold Anchor Steam it is.

T rying to determine who brewed the first beer in California is a bit like asking who discovered America—it depends on who you ask. We can state with some assurance, though, that the first beer makers in the territory would have come from the same tradition of Native American brewers and vintners who were making *chicha, pulque,* and various wild fruit wines across the southwestern portion of what today is the United States.

As for the first European-style brewers, though, it's well worth remembering that long before Hollywood and the Beach Boys came along, California was part of the Mexican Republic. And in Mexico, Hispanic brewers were making New World beer a full century prior to the arrival of the Pilgrims. When the conquistador Hernán Cortés landed in

Anchor's legendary brewmaster, Mark Carpenter, tending to a batch in the early 1970s. By sticking to traditional methods and remaining comparatively small, the company became one of the country's first craft breweries without even realizing it. They were just trying to make great beer.

Mexico in 1519, hell-bent on conquering the Aztecs in the name of Spain, he did so with an entourage of Spanish soldiers who knew how to make beer. Barley-based beer had long been brewed in Iberia—it had been made by Celto-Iberians for centuries prior to the arrival of the Romans in the peninsula, and there exists at least a theory that the word *cerveza,* adopted early by the Romans in Spain, has its origins in the ancient Celtic word for the drink. Cortés's men may have been predominantly wine drinkers, but they consumed beer as well, and according to some accounts, did attempt

to make it in limited quantities. Any barley brewing that occurred in Mexico would have been small-scale, at least until
1542, when a district governor named Don Alonso de Herrero
was granted a twenty-year license by Emperor Carlos V to
brew beer in the city of Nájara. Ultimately, though, it seems
Señor Herrero faced the same problems his brewing brethren
faced in the English colonies just a bit farther north: barley
wasn't easy to grow in the warm Mexican climate, and any
beer produced faced stiff competition from imported forms of
tariff-protected alcohol. Domestic, European-style beer never
thrived in Mexico during the colonial period, and the bulk of
the beer produced would have been of the Native American
variety. When both Baja California and Alta California were
added to the empire of New Spain in the late eighteenth century, the pattern continued in those lands as well.

California's barley-beer drought would come to an end,
though, with the arrival of the gringos. Even before the United
States strong-armed its southern neighbor into handing over
California in 1848 as a result of the Mexican-American War,
Anglo-Americans had been wiggling their way into the terri-
tory and bringing their taste for beer right along with them.
There is a legend, widely known although difficult to verify,
that "Billy the Brewer," purportedly a sailor named William
McGlove, was making beer in California as early as 1837.
And by 1843, bottled beer was definitely being shipped into
the territory via ports for the first round of cautious settlers.
These would have been small amounts of beer, though, for a
relatively small number of beer-drinking newcomers.

Then, on January 24, 1848, everything changed. On that
day, a humble foreman named James W. Marshall, working
on the construction of a lumber mill at the mangy outpost of
Coloma, California, noticed something sparkly in the water
below. There was gold in them thar' hills. His boss, John

Sutter, sought to keep the news quiet, but failed in spectacular fashion. Within no time at all, a newspaper publisher by the name of Samuel Brannan had set up a prospecting supply store and was shouting through the streets of San Francisco at the top of his lungs: "Gold! Gold! Gold from the American River!" U.S. troops already occupied Alta California as the spoils of war; it was officially ceded to the United States in the Treaty of Guadalupe Hidalgo less than two weeks after the discovery. It didn't take long for the news to travel back east, with the *New York Herald* breaking the story that same summer. The California Gold Rush was officially under way, spurred on by the same conviction that would eventually lure everyone from Dust Belt Oklahomans to aspiring Hollywood starlets to try their luck in the golden West: California was a land of opportunity.

California changed drastically, and fast—to the detriment of the Mexicans and Native Americans who already called it home. At the start of the Mexican-American War in 1846, there were a mere 7,000 citizens of the United States living in the territory. By 1850, that number had boomed to a staggering 100,000. So rapid was its settlement and so promising its future, California became a state that same year. "Manifest Destiny," the expansionist's dream of a country that stretched from sea to shining sea, had become a reality faster than anyone could imagine. Gold veins were tapped, timberlines were cut, and Americans poured in like a human river. A prospector's account from 1852, written near the Auburn Ravine in Placer County, gives some sense of the unbelievable growth:

> When we came here, about six weeks ago there were only one or two tents in sight, and in one short week our tent is in the centre of a town, with six stores, two blacksmith

shops, Drug stores, Taverns, Bakery, Circus etc. Verily, California is a go-ahead country.

The first settlers may have been content with circuses and bakeries for a time, but brewers were never far behind. In 1849, the Empire Brewery, at Second Street near Mission, was already turning out beer to the thirsty prospectors of San Francisco. That same year, a newcomer by the name of Mary Jane Megquier would write to her daughter back east, describing in detail a "nice thanksgiving dinner," complete with copious amounts of porter and ale. That fact that they were drinking this instead of lager is not unexpected—in the 1840s, the more established English-style beers still maintained their hegemony in the American brewing scene and would continue to be prominent well into the 1850s. By 1852, San Francisco was alleged to have had 350 barrooms around the city, which meant in a town with a population of 36,000, there was roughly one legal saloon for every hundred people—reportedly one of the largest proportionate number of drinking establishments in the country. In terms of selection, the saloons ran the gamut, from the gilded gambling parlors of Portsmouth Square, to the cheapest and tawdriest of back-alley brothels. In places like the Bella Union and the El Dorado—which were definitely the former—the would-be gambler was greeted by baroque furniture, crystal chandeliers, mirrors of fine cut glass, and a host of attractive waitresses keeping time to a polished melodeon. In the dives of the Barbary Coast a short walk away, he would be just as likely to encounter a bucket of rotgut whiskey, some pretty rough customers, and a punch on the nose. But overall, thanks to its location as a port city, San Francisco attracted a more diverse crowd of migrants, and with it, a more diverse menu of drinks than many saloons in the American West. "Hail to the

San Franciscan," one contemporary extolled, "whose cool climate both fosters a desire for liquor and enables him to carry it." The drink list of one California grog shop from 1850—a full 110 items long—lists such diverse options as Portuguese Port, French Champagne, Jamaica Rum, Holland Gin, Spanish Sack, and host of bizarre cocktails one rarely if ever encounters today. Tog, Smasher, Ching Ching, Vox Populi, Tug and Try . . . apparently all were big hits in Gold Rush–era San Francisco. In fact, a drink called Pisco Punch, made with Peruvian brandy, would go on to become the most popular libation of the day. Its recipe too has been lost to the ages, but one drinker remembered its main ingredient as follows:

> It is perfectly colourless, quite fragrant, very seductive, terribly strong, and has a flavor somewhat resembling that of Scotch whiskey, but much more delicate, with a marked fruity taste. It comes in earthen jars, broad at the top and tapering down to a point, holding about five gallons each. We had some hot, with a bit of lemon and a dash of nutmeg, in it . . . The first glass satisfied me that San Francisco was a nice place to visit . . . The second glass was sufficient, and I felt that I could face small-pox, all the fevers known to the faculty, and the Asiatic cholera, combined, if need be.

Fancy cocktails and gilded saloons were obviously available for the upper echelons of San Francisco society. But for the average San Franciscan struggling to make ends meet while gambling away his gold dust, far more quotidian fare awaited, served at simple saloons with rough wood interiors. And while whiskey, with its lack of refrigeration and indefinite shelf life, was always the simpler choice, beer was also a popular drink. Many of said bars were, as one observer noted, "second-rate

English drinking-shops" where a committed patron could "swig his ale." But the propensity for top-fermenting brews was not to last. Bottom-fermenting lager yeast came with the Germans, and with its crisper, more refreshing flavor, it didn't take very much time for it to win over converts in a place where the workdays were long, sweaty, and inevitably parching. In 1857, an Industrial Exhibition held in the city featured nine breweries, six of which produced porter and ale, and three of which were brewing lager. But by the close of the decade, lager yeast beer appears to have lapped the competition. Eighteen seventy-five is often given as the year of the first true cold-conditioned lager in California; however, historical records seem to indicate that the Bavarian style of beer arrived in the state very soon after its founding, albeit minus the extended time in an ice-cooled cellar. True, the Eagle Brewery and the Eureka Brewery would continue to make beer in the Anglo-American fashion, but they were soon eclipsed in San Francisco by their Teutonic rivals. The Philadelphia Brewery, the California Brewery, the San Francisco Brewery, the Bavarian Brewery—they were all captained by industrious Germans. A general lack of mechanical refrigeration did mean, however, that lager beers were forced to ferment and mature quickly, and at more ale-friendly temperatures. But German brewers were an obstinate lot—the idea that they could subsist for two decades in the Bay Area with nothing more than English-style ale to drink is not only implausible, but simply untrue.

The German thirst for lager produced an innovation out west, even if it came about by accident. By using lager yeasts in a more temperate, winterless, ale-conducive climate, the early brewers of San Francisco and its environs inadvertently created a distinctive style of West Coast beer—a hybrid, if you will, called "steam beer." As for the name, there are contending theories to place its origin. One popular explanation states that the "steam" comes from the large metallic cooling vats, or coolships, that once stood atop many brewery roofs. Without ice or refrigeration, brewers often resorted to this measure as the most effective means of lowering the temperature of the freshly boiled wort prior to pitching the yeast. In the crisp evening breezes that came off the Pacific, this inevitably created steam—hence the name. The theory certainly is plausible, although it neglects to mention that rooftop coolships were not unique to California, and any steam witnessed would have been seen by only a very few people in the brewery's immediate vicinity. A more plausible explanation is that the "steam" actually comes from the pressure that built up inside kegs, thanks to the combined effects of a warmer California climate and the popular practice of kräusening barrels. The latter, as the reader may recall, was a technique for improving the clarity and carbonation of beer in the keg, somewhat akin to the champagne method. But as anyone who has ever tapped a warm keg at a summer barbecue can tell you, when refrigeration isn't available, things get messy. And at a time in American history when steam power was all the rage, it's not surprising that a burst of foam and a hiss of vapor from a newly tapped barrel might be equated with the new technology.

Steam beer was a fast, convenient way to make a lager-style beer available in somewhat difficult circumstances. Lager *style*, mind you, because although it was made with lager yeast, there was generally no actual cold-conditioning or lagering involved. "Steam beer is allowed from ten to twelve days from the mash tub to the glass," according to a beer drinker writing in 1898, meaning that a fresh batch was never more than a few weeks away—useful in the growing West, where a town's population could virtually double overnight. Steam beer generally wasn't of the highest quality—it did have something of a blue-collar reputation—but it was, according to that same writer, better than the alternative. "It is a pretty fair drink," he went on to say. "At any rate, it tastes better than the raw hopped, bitter and turbid ales." A decent way, it seems, to keep at least a form of lager available, at a time when icehouses and refrigeration were not easy to come by in the City by the Bay.

San Francisco was the primary hub of beer making in California, but it wasn't the only brewing city in the far West. In fact, Sacramento followed right on its neighbor's malty heels. Sacramento's population doubled between 1850 and 1855, and with that growth came a healthy expansion in brewing. By 1855, the burgeoning town could claim five breweries to its name, capable of producing a total of 225 barrels a week. Nearby Stockton had a brewery as early as 1851, a facility that was, according to one report, powered by a windmill, but burned down on Christmas Eve of 1857. And of course, there's Los Angeles—the city never acquired the same reputation for brewing as its northern neighbors, but it did have at least one beer-making outfit as early as 1854, when a Christopher Kuhn established a brewery there. Outside these growing urban centers, breweries also appeared in the peculiar collection of mining towns and trading posts that seemed to spring up, and then vanish again, with equal rapidity. Most of them, by the 1860s and 1870s, were captained by German brewers, and given the hardscrabble conditions and lack of cooling available, were likely brewing some early variant of California steam beer.* Generally, though, the farther south

---

*Today, the Anchor Brewing Company owns the trademark on "Steam Beer," which has resulted in the name "California Common" to be more commonly used in the industry. This may be frustrating for some newcomers, but after sticking it out all those years, it's probably safe to say that the old San Francisco brewery has earned it.

one ventured, the less likely one would be to find very much beer, due to climate, ingredients, and demographics.

North, however, was a different story altogether. Not just in Northern California, where beer abounded, but in the new Oregon Territory as well. By the time the border was finally established separating Oregon from Crown-controlled Canada in 1846, there were already several thousand Americans calling the Pacific Northwest their home. And as it soon became apparent, the city of Portland loved its beer then just as it does today. Early brewers included a Mr. Henry Saxer, who founded a brewery in 1852, and John Meany, who opened a successful brewery just across the Columbia River, to be hailed by some as "the leading brewer of the coast north of San Francisco." Meany was eventually bought out by one of his assistants, an ambitious upstart named Henry Weinhard, who had done the traditional German immigrant hopscotch, going first to Philadelphia, then on to Cincinnati, later St. Louis, and eventually the West Coast. Weinhard ran a successful business, outsold his primary competitors, and assumed his predecessor's mantle as the lead brewer in the region north of San Francisco.

Which, incidentally, was also where Henry Weinhard bought his malt and hops. In the decades following the Gold Rush, the top half of California had become a barley and hops powerhouse. According to one historian, California "produced in average years nearly as much barley as wheat, and in some seasons, even more." Hops flourished in the temperate northern climate as well, which meant that beer was able to remain a local product. The conditions might not have been great for natural lagering, but they were superb—especially in the higher altitudes and in the cool shaded valleys—for producing the primary ingredients in beer. Barley and hops didn't need to be shipped in from the farming centers in the Upper Midwest or Upstate New

Washington State's Yakima Valley became the center for hop production in America and ensured that West Coast breweries always had a source nearby.

York—they could be grown much closer to home. By the turn of the twentieth century, the American hop industry was essentially based out of the Pacific Northwest, with the Yakima Valley in Washington destined to become the hop capital of the world. With beer being produced both inexpensively and locally, that also meant that imported beer from the brewing behemoths of St. Louis and Milwaukee would face some stiff competition—at least for a time. The macrobrews certainly had their eyes on the coast, but for a while—more than half a century, in fact—cities like San Francisco and Portland were part of a unique and truly regional brew culture, one that produced its own distinctive styles of bottom-fermenting beer, using locally grown barley and northwestern hops. The arrival of widespread mechanical refrigeration in the late nineteenth century meant that true, cold-

Brewing in the early days of San Francisco was a decidedly scrappy affair. Refrigeration was scarce, hours were long, and conditions could be primitive. But locals did whatever was necessary to keep the taps open.

conditioned lager could at last be made on America's West Coast. But steam beer had secured its place in the heart of a region and would continue to be a mainstay of the California saloon—that is until the Big One hit.

For most Americans, the date April 18, 1906, is not especially noteworthy or momentous. But for San Franciscans, it can still summon an ominous shudder. Because at 5:12 A.M., a 7.8 magnitude earthquake nearly shook the city out of existence. The tremblor didn't last long, but the destruction it unleashed would obliterate much of the town. Between collapses and resulting fires, nearly 80 percent of San Francisco was destroyed, and some three thousand people lost their lives. Three-quarters of the population became homeless refugees in a manner of minutes, while whole neighborhoods were razed to the ground and entire industries almost ceased to exist—including the brewing industry. This account of one brewery destroyed by the earthquake, published just one year after the disaster, gives some sense of just how structurally vulnerable many of the hastily constructed facilities actually were:

> The plant of the Jackson Brewing Company, on the southeast corner of Eleventh and Folsom streets, was in [the] process of construction and was wrecked by the earthquake, the damage by fire being but slight. The brick walls were laid in lime mortar of poor quality. The steel beams and girders were supported by cast-iron columns. Many of the various steel members were bolted together with an insufficient number of bolts, the girders and beams resting upon walls without any tie; the columns, girders, and beams were not fireproofed, and in the eastern half the concrete floor slabs, 6 inches thick, were without reinforcement. Several persons were killed by the collapse of the tower. That this building should have been wrecked is not surprising, as the design was bad and the material and workmanship were very poor.

The Jackson Brewing Company was not the only beer maker that lost everything. According to one report, written by Theodore Rueger of the Benicia Brewery for the *American Brewer's Review,* of the twenty-five breweries operating in San Francisco prior to the quake, fourteen were either badly damaged or totally destroyed, including the Willows Brewery, the Wreden Brewery, the Albany Brewery, and the Anchor Brewery. "Words cannot describe or picture show half the ruin and desolation wrought by the flames and earthquake," he lamented, although his brewery-by-brewery account does

The San Francisco earthquake of 1906 didn't just reduce much of the city's architecture to rubble—it almost destroyed the city's brewing industry, as demonstrated by the ruins of a brewery pictured above.

paint a vivid picture. His friends at Anchor, it seems, got the very worst of it: "when we came there," he wrote in his damage report, "we saw a [brew] kettle standing on the side of a hill, the only thing to indicate that the Anchor Brewery had been there." But despite the devastation, he would also note that "the spirit of the people is not broken, and from this scene of crumbled walls will grow a better city."

The city did recover. And the Anchor Brewery, although hobbled by the earthquake of 1906, would rebuild, opening a new location south of Market Street the very next year. But while many breweries did reopen, the brewing industry of the West Coast's beer capital would never be the same. World War I would severely hinder brewing a mere decade later, and Prohibition would prove as disastrous for the breweries of the West Coast as it was for beer producers back east—in some cases, even more so. Unlike the large breweries of the Midwest and the East Coast, many local facilities lacked the refrigeration capacity necessary to switch production to ice cream and soft drinks—unable to adapt, most went under. And for the handful of West Coast breweries that survived the Volstead Act, by the postwar years, competing with the megabreweries was simply not an option. The few remaining local breweries did get a brief respite during the 1930s and 1940s, when a general leeriness of national advertising campaigns coupled with the substantial cost of shipping kept midwestern beers out of the West Coast markets. In fact, by 1940, California was the tenth-largest beer-consuming state in the Union, with much of that beer produced locally. But by the 1950s, those same megabrands had found a clever solution: build their own breweries on the locals' turf. No longer content to simply ship in their beer via train at a prohibitive cost, most of the leading breweries in the Midwest opened satellite facilities in California to service a boom-

The physical barrier of the Rockies, coupled with a local supply of hops and barley, helped keep the large breweries of the Midwest away from the West Coast and allowed local brands to prosper—at least for a time. By the 1950s, the corporate giants had begun opening their own satellite breweries in California, bringing national brands to what had been a predominantly regional market.

ing postwar population. With many of the old-time brewers unable to refrigerate or package their product as effectively as the big guys, or differentiate themselves in a commercially viable way, they had no way to keep up. The goliaths of the Midwest could prosper in a low-margin, marketing-driven, and increasingly technology-dependent industry, while the local brewers could not.

Between 1947 and 1958, the number of American breweries dropped by 46 percent, from 465 to 252, while the combined market share of the five-largest breweries grew from 21 percent to 31 percent. The transition of beer drinking from a saloon-based activity to one centered around the suburban home transformed the industry, with increased investment in bottling and canning equipment, and improvements in preservation technology—hurting smaller, regional brewers that lacked the funds to put money toward either. As a result, the midwestern imports became known as "premium beer," not because of the richness of their malts or the bouquet of their hops, but simply because they were reliably consistent. Back on the East Coast, there were still enough sizable local breweries to at least hold their own—names like Ballantine, Schaefer, Ruppert, and Rheingold. On the West Coast, however, where brewing had always been a smaller and scrappier affair, competing with the imports became less and less feasible. The Los Angeles Brewery, Acme, Rainier, Olympia, and General—the largest local breweries of the West Coast—all put up a fight. But in the end, they could not go up against the juggernaut of Busch, Pabst, Miller, and Schlitz. When the midwestern breweries entered the California market in 1953 and 1954, opening million-barrel facilities across the state, it was essentially game over. Their biggest competition came, in fact, not from the locals, but from the mountain brewers at Coors, who already had extensive experience distributing beer all over the West.

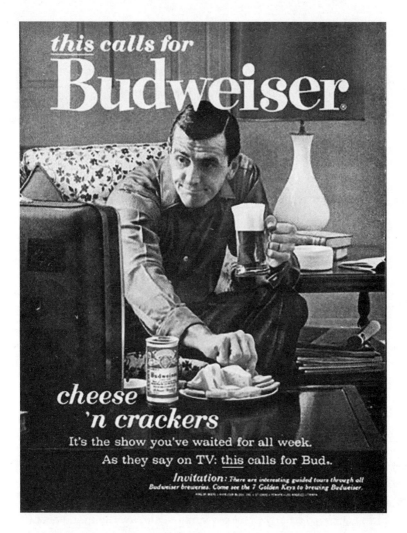

The rise of the suburbs in the 1950s and 1960s was reflected in our nation's beer preferences. Breweries increasingly marketed their product to a suburban audience, one that preferred to enjoy modern products in the comfort of their own homes.

By the early 1960s, the rise of the American beer oligopoly was essentially complete. For the big-four breweries of the Midwest, competition was no longer aimed at local producers—who had already lost any advantages they had in regard to regional distribution—but at each other. They would jockey for position in the decades that followed with national marketing campaigns and sale-enhancing innovations. In an age when American foodstuffs were trading in flavor for profitability—just look at white bread, American cheese, or instant coffee—American beer followed suit. Seemingly everything was watered down and overhyped, and domestic beer was no exception. "Light Beer," introduced to the mass market in the 1970s as a less-filling, low-calorie alternative to conventional brews, coincided nicely with the arrival of fad diets and disco crazes and cemented the notion of what good beer should be: refreshing, bland, and easy to drink. The pilsner-style pale lager introduced to the American market in the nineteenth century had become, by the latter decades of the twentieth, a wan shadow of its former self. The 1980s saw Spuds McKenize, the Bud Bowl, and the Swedish Bikini Team all cartoonishly promoting mass-produced beer to a general audience whose taste in beverages was not exactly what one might call sophisticated. By 1983, only forty-three brewing firms operated in the United States—this, in a nation that prior to Prohibition, boasted well over a thousand. And in the decade that followed, the market share of the four-largest breweries would swell to over 80 percent—up from less than 10 percent in the first decade of the twentieth century. There just didn't seem to be any place for small-scale, locally made beer in a country that liked its drinks cold, convenient, and served in a can. Thankfully, the microbrew obituary would prove premature. Unbeknownst to anyone, a revolution was already brewing, and the West Coast was where it would all begin.

When the Mamas & the Papas released their 1965 hit, "California Dreamin'," the group was expressing far more than a longing for sunshine and palm trees.

They were providing the soundtrack to a generation of young Americans, and giving voice to the first rumblings of a counterculture that was rapidly expanding beyond the bohemian enclaves of big cities, and becoming something of a national movement. Mama Cass wasn't the only one pining for California—the youth of America was getting the itch to ditch the suburbs and go out west, and the nexus of it all seemed to be the City on the Bay. From Jack London to Jack Kerouac, San Francisco had always been a destination for those seeking the freedom to explore new ideas and live in unconventional ways. Perhaps it was because of its unique history—both as a cosmopolitan port and a frontier outpost—it had served since the beginning as a haven for individuals from diverse backgrounds looking to try their hand at something new. Whatever the reason, the city and the band both struck a common chord. Just two years later, when Scott McKenzie crooned, "If you're going to San Francisco, be sure to wear some flowers in your hair," the town had become all but a mecca for those wishing to experience alternative lifestyles. *Flower power* and *free love* became the words of the day, as adherents to new philosophies rejected what they saw as the military-industrial complex, and all the mass-produced conformity that went along with it.

To be sure, the counterculture movement that blossomed in California had its unsavory side—rampant drug use, cult-like communes, and, lest we forget, one terribly creepy guy named Charles Manson. But it certainly had its positive aspects as well, all of which contributed greatly to causes like civil rights, world peace, and gender equality. Those hippies may have had some peculiar notions of hair length and hem width, but their idealism helped guide American values in a time when a moral compass was sorely needed. Including, although it gets significantly less attention than those other causes, the value we placed on consumer goods. Coupled with their rejection of corporate greed and cultural conformity was a desire to explore older, more traditional ways of producing staples. Suddenly, many were wondering if perhaps it was better to grow your own organic vegetables than to buy them from a factory farm. If it was wiser, possibly, to knit your own sweater from homespun wool instead of shipping it in from a sweatshop in Asia. A little naive, maybe, but they were raising some important questions.

Many young Californians became interested in getting back to the land with a "do it yourself" mentality. Guides like *The Foxfire Book* taught lost arts such as cabin building and folk healing to children of the suburbs, and troubadours like Woody Guthrie and Pete Seeger exposed a fresh new crop of listeners to the old folk tunes of the American canon. In the postwar years, Americans had embraced wholeheartedly the glitz and glamour of the atomic age. Keeping up with the Joneses meant buying sleek, mass-produced products that were convenient and uniform above all else. By the late '60s, however, the baby boomers who had grown up in that era were left wondering if that quest for modernity and convenience had even been worth it. If maybe, just maybe, we had lost a big part of ourselves in the process.

One California transplant who embraced the ethos of "bigger isn't always better" was the very Frederick "Fritz" Maytag mentioned in the beginning of this chapter—a young man who also happened to be, somewhat ironically, the direct descendant of the founder of the Maytag Washing Machine Company. After graduating from Stanford and bouncing around several unfulfilling jobs, he came to San Francisco, as so many of his generation did, to collect his thoughts and figure out what, exactly, he wanted out of life. By 1965, he

still hadn't quite figured it out, although he knew he appreciated the distinct character and history of the city, along with
some of its historic bohemian haunts—one of which was the
Old Spaghetti Factory, a place known more for the price of its
beer than the quality of its pasta. Fritz became friendly with
the owner and fond of the only brew it had on tap: Anchor
Steam Beer, a peculiar relic from the old days, when early San
Francisco brewers had to make their lager yeast concoctions
without the benefits of refrigeration. Only, according to said
owner, the brewery was going to go under any day. He urged
the twenty-five-year-old to visit the brewery while he still
could—its days in San Francisco were apparently numbered.

Fritz didn't just visit the insolvent brewery—he ended up
buying it, for "less than the price of a used car," as he would
later recall. He had no brewing experience, but he had business acumen and an appreciation for craft. He had grown up
on his father's dairy farm back in Iowa, famous for its traditionally made European-style cheeses, and he understood the
importance of proper ingredients and attention to detail. It was
quality, not quantity, he reckoned, that would keep his new
brewery alive. "I want to make all our beer in this building—
hands on," he insisted. "I mean this: we do not—emphatically
do not—want to get too big." An American entrepreneur who
specifically wanted to keep his operation small? At the time,
the idea wasn't just unorthodox, it was practically treasonous.

It took years to turn a profit, and serious investment in
equipment and training, but this new philosophy began to pay
off. Maytag returned his Anchor Steam Beer to its original
nineteenth century pure-barley recipe, tinkered with ways to
lengthen its shelf life without unsavory preservatives, and capitalized on the beer's unique heritage: "Made in San Francisco
since 1896," stated the label, which was accurate, but also
humble. Truth be told, the company's origins went all the way

A young Fritz Maytag enjoys an Anchor Steam Beer circa 1965. In saving a relic from San Francisco's golden age of brewing, he also helped restore craftsmanship and individuality to American beer—not to mention inspire a whole generation of ambitious young brewers, both in the West and the East.

back to the Gold Rush, when a German Forty-Eighter named Gottlieb Brekle decided to become a Forty-Niner. But 1896 was the year that the name "Anchor" was first attached to the beer, and that became the official date. By the mid-1970s, the brand was picking up steam, no pun intended, and many could feel, if not come out and say, that something was changing— the tide was turning. Suddenly that old-timey beer with the funny labels was starting to look *and* taste more appealing than the canned Middle American brews that still dominated the store aisles. The addition of a "Liberty Ale" to the Anchor repertoire to commemorate Paul Revere's ride just before the bicentennial not only brought a practically defunct style of yeast back to the American brewing scene, it also included a new variety of local Cascade hop from the Yakima Valley, just to the north. At the time it was no great shakes, but the first

The entire Anchor staff in 1978—a group of people who obviously enjoyed their work. The craft beer revolution didn't begin in corporate offices or boardrooms, but in small, local breweries like this.

small rumblings of something far bigger were beginning to shake the foundations of America's beer establishment.

As it turned out, Fritz Maytag wasn't the only one in California intrigued by the notion of brewing a high-quality, small-scale beer. But while he had put his plan into action by purchasing an existing local brewery, a man named Jack McAuliffe actually had the novel idea of starting his own *original* microbrewery and producing his own original beer. It all started, interestingly enough, in Scotland, a long ways away from the sunny shores of the Golden State. While stationed there during a stint in the U.S. Navy in the '60s, he had discovered what locally made, Old World beer tasted like, and had taken it upon himself to try making his own. Home brewing was just taking off in the United Kingdom, thanks to the lifting of a licensing law that had been on the books for eighty years. It didn't happen right away, but eventually McAuliffe was able to turn out a brew that fellow servicemen and locals alike were more than happy to imbibe. And when he returned to the States, fully aware that the traditional British-style ales he had become accustomed to would no longer be available except as expensive imports, he decided to take his kit and his skills with him back across the pond. Settling in California, ostensibly to attend school, he also discovered that the abundance of wine-making supply stores that catered to the vineyards surrounding the Bay Area could just as readily supply much-needed brewing equipment. When a chef named Alice Waters opened the legendary restaurant Chez Panisse nearby, using local ingredients and gourmet methods to prepare her food, something clicked. Between the resurgence of Anchor Steam Beer, the growth of a respected local wine industry, and the arrival of a new food culture that valued quality and tradition, the table appeared to be set for something new. With help from investors Suzy Stern and Jane Zimmerman, he opened the New Albion Brewing Company in 1976, in Sonoma, California—ground zero for the explosive new American food and drink movement that was taking hold in the region. They would go on to brew a wide variety of porters and ales, and lobby for laws that would eventually allow breweries to serve food and alcohol on premises, essentially paving the way for the arrival of brewpubs.

New Albion closed after six years, despite some national press and a solid reputation—perhaps it was just a touch too far ahead of its time. But its legacy was profound. In 1978, America lifted an old Prohibition-era ban on homemade beer, enabling many others to pursue their passion for brewing quality ale. With making beer at home no longer a federal crime, home-brew enthusiasts were able to come up from their basements and practice in the open—including a western transplant and nuclear engineer named Charlie Papazian. As the home brewers stepped out of the shadows and revealed themselves, Papazian and his brewing buddy Charlie Matzen formed the American Homebrewers Association to better serve their interests. The AHA brought new disciples to the cause and helped spread the gospel of good beer by publishing a number of home-brewing guides, some of which are still used by hobbyists to this day.

In 1979, just one year after legalization, a pair of California home brewers named Ken Grossman and Paul Camusi decided to turn their formerly illicit hobby into a business, founding the Sierra Nevada Brewing Co. in the town of Chico, just a little ways north of Sacramento. To get their venture off the ground, they relied on advice from fellow brewers Fritz Maytag, Jack McAuliffe, and Charlie Papazian. Far from being competitors, they were instead collaborators in the same cause—to bring high-quality beer back to America. And all that collaboration paid off with the release soon after of the trailblazing Sierra Nevada Pale Ale, as well as a subsequent India Pale Ale—an even maltier, hoppier style first developed by the British to survive the long, hot journey to colonial India. However, by using a high dose of whole American Cascade hops, robust malts, and bottle conditioning, they essentially created a new West Coast style of craft beer. And they proved that an original, small-scale brewery could actually be commercially viable—the company produced 950 barrels of beer in its first year, and doubled its output in the year that followed. By 1983, it was turning out some 30 barrels a week. Not huge numbers, certainly, but there was steady growth. This new style of locally made ale was selling, and in no time, other "microbreweries" were cropping up across the northern half of the state, all seeking to duplicate Sierra Nevada's success. The first tremors of the craft beer revolution were already starting to rattle the West Coast drinking scene.

And they didn't stop at the state line. North of California in Oregon and Washington, the Pacific Northwest was experiencing a brewing renaissance of its own, building on a century-old tradition of using locally grown barley and hops. A Portland beer evangelist named Fred Eckhardt—also an acquaintance of Anchor's Fritz Maytag—had long been advocating for a return to traditional, carefully made brews. His self-published journals and brewing guides catered to home brewers, expounding the importance of craft when it came to making beer—and folks started to listen. As early as 1980, Charles and Shirley Coury of Portland were selling a light ale from their Cartwright Brewery for one dollar a bottle. The brewery ran into fiscal hardship and did not last, but other Oregon brewers picked up the baton, including the Columbia River Brewery and the Widmer Brothers Brewing Company. And farther north yet, the Redhook Ale Brewery was turning out West Coast–style ale to the thirsty people of Seattle starting in 1981. Like morels after a soft spring rain, microbreweries were springing up across Northern California and the Pacific Northwest both. It had experienced a few hurdles at the start, but the craft beer movement was picking up steam.

All that was needed was someone to take this new notion of "good beer" and introduce it to the American public at large. By the early '80s, craft beer existed in America, but it was still a niche product—something to be found in a few obscure specialty stores in a few discreet corners of the country. Defined by a smaller size, more traditional methods, and independent ownership, craft breweries were easily overshadowed by the macrobrews that dominated the supermarket shelves and media airwaves. To most people in the United States, "beer" still meant a beverage that was served in a can and nearly clear as water. Malt, yeast, and hops were all secondary considerations. What was needed was that special someone with the proper pedigree, an appreciation for craft, and a little marketing savvy. After all, convincing an entire generation raised on light beer to embrace something darker, richer, and more complex was hardly a walk in the park. A new way of making and selling craft beer was needed.

Fortunately, the West Coast beer community didn't have to wait long for its message to go mainstream. In 1984, some three thousand miles and a full beer book's worth of history away, a young Jim Koch, inspired by the spirit of those early pioneers, used his own family's long-forgotten recipe to create Samuel Adams Boston Lager. In doing so, he took what had been a local movement and introduced it to the American people, ushering in a true renaissance of local and regional beer. By 1990, the number of American breweries had increased to nearly three hundred. By 1995, it stood closer to a thousand. And by the turn of the twenty-first century, American breweries, which had numbered only in the dozens just a few decades before, were more than fifteen hundred strong. The tide had turned and the nation was changing, with something new to the beer scene appearing every day. Harpoon, Dogfish Head, 90 Minute IPAs, Imperial Stouts, Brooklyn, San Diego, Russian River, Pliny the Younger . . . well, you know the rest.

And the rest, as they say, is history.

IN BEER WE TRUST

THIS BOOK BEGAN WITH A QUESTION—ONE THAT CAME TO light while I was waiting for my first batch of home brew to cool in our nation's capital. How did beer, a beverage both essential and, for most of its existence, undeniably local, shape the regional histories of this country? Surely, such a valued product must have figured into the identities of what really is more a conglomeration of cultures than any monolithic state. The beloved brewdog must have played a pivotal role in defining how we, as northerners, southerners, midwesterners, and westerners, define ourselves.

It seemed simple enough at the time, chatting with my brother-in-law Steve on a beautiful day with a half-dozen beers already under our belts. But now, with things coming to an end almost three hundred pages later, it might be best to close with a confession: it took a whole lot longer than the few weeks I envisioned to find the answers. And, frankly, I'm still finding them. American history is an evolving story, and our understanding of it is malleable to the facts at hand. No sooner had I finished up my description of the sad demise of the English alewife in the 1500s, when I happened to stumble upon an English cooking manual from 1615, which listed "brewing" among the skills to be mastered by the lady of the manor—proof that at least some English women were still carrying on a tradition that would eventually bring pumpkin beer to New England and molasses brews to the southern colonies. And I didn't discover this while digging through microfiche in some musty archive; I was just Googling a pancake recipe on a Sunday morning. History, like beer, is all around us. Crack it open, and you're never sure exactly what you're going to get, although chances are, if it's consumed thoughtfully and discerningly, it will make for an enjoyable experience.

One thing I can say with certainty, however, after having spent a solid year of studious sampling, is this: there has never been a better time to be a beer drinker in America. This book started with the premise that the richness of the American experience has always sprung from our own diversity, and at this moment, the brewing culture in the United States is as diverse as it has ever been. When Jack McAuliffe opened the first new craft brewery in America since Prohibition in the late '70s, there were fewer than fifty breweries operating in the United States. When Jim Koch cooked up his first batch of Boston Lager in 1984, there were still less than a hundred. But today, just a few decades later, there are well over three *thousand*. And within all those permutations of yeast, malt, and hops lies an almost unlimited potential for truly great beer, no matter one's personal preference. For those looking to taste heritage in a glass, there are the old-school breweries that survived Prohibition and still make traditional styles of lager—places like Yuengling, Shiner, and Anchor Steam. If it's pushing the envelope you're after, the mad geniuses at breweries like Dogfish Head, Stone, and Rogue are always looking to combine age-old techniques with bold innovations—Dogfish actually produced a stout made with chocolate, lobster, and basil, should you need convincing. And for nostalgia, or even just simple refreshment, there's always the assortment of macrobrews we all grew up on. Sure, they might get a bad rap from the connoisseurs, but it's also well worth remembering that when America nearly became a country of whiskey drinkers in the nineteenth century, and cocktail drinkers in the twentieth, it was Messrs. Busch, Schlitz, and Pabst who pulled us back from the brink. They effectively saved American beer, and we might not be drinking it at all were it not for them.[*]

The future of regional beer is harder to divine, but we can certainly speculate. Some in the industry have voiced concerns about market saturation, although small-scale independent brewing at a local level will likely continue to grow for the foreseeable future, if recent trends are anything to go on. In 2013, Americans even managed to drink more craft beer than Budweiser—a feat unimaginable just a few years before. Inevitably, though, we still go back to what we already know, and certain proclivities lend themselves to rediscovering old favorites. As a country, we may be exploring new ways to drink our beer, but our regional roots run deep indeed. Malty,

---

[*]Also, it seems that history is not without its own sense of irony. After more than a century of big breweries outselling or buying out the regional "little guys," some of the biggest beer brands in America have themselves been purchased by heavy hitters from abroad. At the time of writing, Budweiser, Miller, and Pabst are owned by huge conglomerates based in Belgium, England, and Russia, respectively.

high-alcohol brews made with copious local hops have come to dominate the craft brew scene of the West Coast, just as they did over a hundred years ago. Beers aged in bourbon barrels are gaining popularity in the South, hinting perhaps at some ancestral longing for char and corn, and in New England, seasonal beers have once again become a common sight—apparently, the taste of an autumnal pumpkin ale still holds considerable appeal for the Yankee palate. But that isn't to say that these regional styles don't have national appeal as well (especially when it comes to West Coast IPAs), or that entirely novel forms of beer aren't being created. This heterogeneous nation of ours may have a historic problem with consensus, but it's also never been short on innovation. Just because we embrace the familiar doesn't mean we shy away from creating something new, often in the most unexpected of ways. In the Pacific Northwest, the Cascadian dark ale has arisen from a local love of dark malts and piney hops—and also, according to some, a small but vocal movement to create the independent country of Cascadia. Apparently, the "CDA" is often the local Cascadian separatist's drink of choice. And way over on the other side of the country, the recent obsession with all things "gluten-free" in health-conscious northeastern cities has resulted in some breweries using sorghum syrup rather than barley to make their beer. Little do those antiglutenites know, they're actually drinking a modern, revamped version of a colonial-era molasses beer—the very stuff George Washington and Thomas Jefferson used to brew in their kitchens, making it a great blessing for celiac sufferers and history lovers alike.

And speaking of making beer in the kitchen, my own batch of home brew is finally ready to drink—in fact, my brother-in-law Steve is getting out the glasses right now. No, this isn't the first batch of high-rye IPA that sparked the idea for this book.

That one came out . . . not so good. But while the great midwestern writer F. Scott Fitzgerald may have been right about there being no second acts in American lives, when it comes to American brewing, there's always time for another round.

"All set?" Steve has the bottles uncapped and he's poised for a pour. I nod and take a deep breath. Time for the moment of truth. The instant when I'll finally see if a year's worth of insight can translate into a good batch of brew. With lambent tones of honey and sunlight, laced at the top by a delicate foam, the freshly brewed ale rises in our glasses. It is a thing of wonder and a thing of beauty—happiness in a bottle, history in a glass. We chime rims and take our first tentative sips. For a moment, neither one of us speaks. We let the hops and the alcohol work their bright alchemy. We allow four centuries of the American experience to tingle on the tongue. Words feel all at once superfluous—there really isn't all that much to say—although a shared glance reveals that we're both in agreement. The verdict is?

Well, let's just say we're probably not going to be opening a craft brewery in the near future, and we won't be quitting our day jobs anytime soon. But we did make some very drinkable beer. And as every brewer from Geronimo on down to Jim Koch could tell you, that's something any American can be proud of—no matter where in this sprawling nation of ours he or she is from.

So I'll drink to that.

Cheers.

The author's brother-in-law Steve, engaging with his son Graham in a distinctly midwestern form of father-son bonding.

ACKNOWLEDGMENTS

Books are a collaborative effort, and beer books, I have found, even more so—this one would never have been possible without the help of some amazing people. I'd like to offer a heartfelt thank-you and a hearty cheers to my agent, Jim Fitzgerald, my editor, Peter Hubbard, and his assistant editor, Nick Amphlett, all of whom were instrumental in making this project come to life. Also, a special thanks to Jim Koch and Ashley Leduc of the Boston Beer Company, Mark Carpenter of the Anchor Brewing Company, Josh Jones of the Hofbräuhaus Cleveland, and Dr. Patrick McGovern of the University of Pennsylvania, all of whom took time from their busy schedules to offer their insights and expertise. As for research assistance, MacKenzie Gibson proved ever helpful in digging up obscure documents and academic publications. Additionally, I owe a tremendous debt to my brother-in-law Steve O'Neal, who proved to be a great teacher of the brewing arts, as well as my dad, who first introduced me to the midwestern sacrament of malt and hops. And lastly, much love and gratitude to my wife, Sophie, who has managed to be most forgiving of a burgeoning beer belly. I'll fit in my pants again soon, baby, I promise.

BIBLIOGRAPHY

PROLOGUE: E PLURIBUS, BREWDOG

2013 Brewer's Almanac. Published by The Beer Institute. www .beerinstitute.org

Standage, Tom. *A History of the World in 6 Glasses.* New York: Bloomsbury, 2005.

Gately, Iain. *Drink: A Cultural History.* New York: Gotham Books, 2008.

Hughes, P. S., and E. D. Baxter. *Beer: Quality, Safety, and Nutritional Aspects.* Cambridge: Royal Society of Chemistry, 2001.

McGovern, Patrick. *Uncorking the Past: The Quest for Wine, Beer, and Other Alcoholic Beverages.* Berkeley: University of California Press, 2009.

CHAPTER 1: NEW ENGLAND

Nelson, Max. *The Barbarian's Beverage: A History of Beer in Ancient Europe.* New York: Routledge, 2008.

Bennett, Judith M. *Ale, Beer, and Brewsters in England: Women's Work in a Changing World, 1300–1600.* New York: Oxford University Press, 1996.

Unger, Richard W. *Beer in the Middle Ages and Renaissance.* Philadelphia: University of Pennsylvania Press, 2004.

Smith, Gregg. *Beer: A History of Suds and Civilization from Mesopotamia to Microbreweries.* New York: Avon Books, 1995.

Bradford, William. *Bradford's History of Plymouth Plantation, 1606–1646.* Edited by Jameson Franklin. New York: Charles Scribner's Sons, 1920.

Fischer, David Hacket. *Albion's Seed: Four British Folkways in America.* New York: Oxford University Press, 1989.

Wood, William. *Wood's New-England's Prospect.* Boston: John Wilson and Son, 1865.

Smith, Gregg. *Beer in America: The Early Years—1587–1840.* Boulder: Siris Books, 1998.

Albertson, Dean. "Liquor in the Planting of New England." *The New England Quarterly,* Vol. 23, No. 4. December 1950.

Salinger, Sharon. *Taverns and Drinking in Early America.* Baltimore: The John Hopkins University Press, 2004.

Harding, Gardner. "Harvard's Twenty-Two Presidents." *The Harvard Illustrated Magazine,* Volume XI, No. 1. Cambridge, 1910.

Hirsch, Corin. *Forgotten Drinks of Colonial New England: From Flips & Rattle-Skulls to Switchel & Spruce Beer.* Charleston: Palate Press, 2014.

Williams, Ian. *Rum: A Social and Sociable History.* New York: Nation Books, 2005.

CHAPTER 2: NEW YORK AND THE MID-ATLANTIC
Steinberg. Dan. "The Yankees Have the Worst Beer List in Baseball." *The Washington Post.* August 11, 2014.

Schluter, Hermann. *The Brewing Industry and the Brewery Worker's Movement in America.* Cincinnati: Published by the International Union of United Brewery Workmen of America, 1910.

Unger, Richard W. *Beer in the Middle Ages and Renaissance.* Philadelphia: University of Pennsylvania Press, 2004.

———. *A History of Brewing in Holland 900–1900: Economy, Technology and the State.* Brill, 2001.

Hornsey, Ian Spencer. *A History of Beer and Brewing*. Cambridge: The Royal Society of Chemistry, 2003.

Baron, Staley. *Brewed in America*. Boston: Little, Brown and Company, 1962.

Kross, Jessica. "If You Will Not Drink with Me, Fight with Me: The Sociology of Drinking in the Middle Colonies." *Pennsylvania History*, Vol. 64, No. 1. Penn State University Press, 1997.

The Colonial Laws of New York from the Year 1664 to the Revolution. Clark, NJ: The Lawbook Exchange, 2006.

Elliot, Jonathan. *The Debates of the Several State Conventions on the Adoption of the Federal Constitution*. Philadelphia: J. B. Lippincott Company, 1891.

CHAPTER 3: THE SOUTH

Harrisse, Henry. *John Cabot: The Discovery of North America, and Sebastian His Son*. London: Benjamin Franklin Stevens, 1896.

Jehlen, Myra, and Michael Warner, eds. *The English Literatures of the America: 1500–1800*. New York: Routledge, 1987.

Geith-Jones, Eric. *George Thorpe and the Berkeley Company*. Gloucester: Alan Sutton Publishing, 1982.

Covey, Herbert, and Dwight Eisnach. *What the Slaves Ate: Recollections of African American Foods and Foodways from Slave Narratives*. Santa Barbara: ABC-Clio, LLC, 2009.

Dunaway, Wilma. *Slavery in the American Mountain South*. Cambridge: Cambridge University Press, 2003.

Fischer, David Hacket. *Albion's Seed: Four British Folkways in America*. New York: Oxford University Press, 1989.

Hirsch, Corin. *Forgotten Drinks of Colonial New England: From Flips & Rattle-Skulls to Switchel & Spruce Beer*. Charleston: Palate Press, 2014.

Baron, Stanley. *Brewed in America: A History of Beer and Ale in the United States.* Boston: Little, Brown and Company, 1962.

McCash, June Hall. *The Jekyll Island Cottage Colony.* Athens: University of Georgia Press, 1998.

Nelson, Max. *The Barbarian's Beverage: A History of Beer in Ancient Europe.* New York: Routledge, 2008.

Fischer, David Hacket. *Albion's Seed: Four British Folkways in America.* New York: Oxford University Press, 1989.

Webb, Jim. *Born Fighting: How the Scots-Irish Shaped America.* New York: Broadway Books, 2004.

Hall, Harrison. *The Distiller.* Philadelphia: Printed by J. Bioren, 1818.

Crowgey, Henry. *Kentucky Bourbon: The Early Days of Whiskeymaking.* Lexington: University of Kentucky Press, 2008.

Rorabaugh, W. J. *The Alcoholic Republic: An American Tradition.* New York: Oxford University Press, 1919.

Ellen, Merrill. *Germans of Louisiana.* Gretna, LA: Pelican Publishing Company, 2005.

Deiler, John Hanno. *Geschichte der New Orleanser deutschen presse.* New Orleans: Gendler Printing Co., 1901.

CHAPTER 4: THE MIDWEST

Nelson, Max. *The Barbarian's Beverage: A History of Beer in Ancient Europe.* New York: Routledge, 2008.

Unger, Richard W. *Beer in the Middle Ages and Renaissance.* Philadelphia: University of Pennsylvania Press, 2004.

Dornbusch, Horst D. *Prost!: The Story of German Beer.* Boulder: Siris Books, 1997.

Oliver, Garrett, ed. *The Oxford Companion to Beer.* New York: Oxford University Press, 2012.

Baron, Stanley. *Brewed in America.* Boston: Little, Brown and Company, 1962.

Mittelman, Amy. *Brewing Battles: A History of American Beer.* New York: Algora Publishing, 2008.

Efford, Alison Clark. *German Immigrants, Race, and Citizenship in the Civil War Era.* New York: Cambridge University Press, 2013.

Burrows, Edwin G., and Mike Wallace. *Gotham: A History of New York to 1889.* New York: Oxford University Press, 1998.

Knoedelseder, William. *Bitter Brew: The Rise and Fall of Anheuser-Busch and America's Kings of Beer.* New York: HarperBusiness, 2012.

Moerman, Daniel E. *Native American Food Plants: An Ethnobotanical Dictionary.* Portland: Timber Press, 2010.

Metzger, Charles H. "Sebastien Louis Meurin: The Last of the Illinois Jesuit Indian Missionaries." *Illinois Catholic Historical Review,* Vol. III, No. 1. July 1920. Chicago: Published by the Illinois Catholic Historical Society, 1920.

Schumacher, Jennifer Watson, ed. *Images of America: German Milwaukee.* Chicago: Arcadia Publishing, 2009.

Appel, Susan K. "Building Milwaukee's Breweries: Pre-Prohibition Brewery architecture in the Cream City." *The Wisconsin Magazine of History,* Vol. 78, No. 3. Spring 1995. Published by the Wisconsin Historical Society.

Rorabaugh, W. J. *The Alcoholic Republic: An American Tradition.* New York: Oxford University Press, 1919.

Mueller, Doris Land. *M. Jeff Thompson: Missouri's Swamp Fix of the Confederacy.* Columbia: University of Missouri Press, 2007.

Lowry, Thomas P. *Irish & German Whiskey & Beer: Drinking Patterns in the Civil War.* Lexington: Published by Thomas P. Lowry, 2011.

Schlutter, Hermann. *The Brewing Industry and the Workers Movement in America.* Cincinnati: Press of Rosenthal & Co., 1910.

Sigsworth, E. M. "Science and the Brewing Industry, 1850–1900." *The Economic History Review,* Vol. 17, No. 3. 1965. Published by the Economic History Society.

Klein, Maury. *The Genesis of Industrial America, 1870–1920.* New York: Cambridge Press, 2007.

CHAPTER 5: THE WEST

Benson, Eric. "The World's Best New Brewery Is in a Strip Mall in Suburban Phoenix." *Esquire Magazine.* April 11, 2014.

La Barre, Weston. "Native American Beers." *American Anthropologist,* Vol. 40, No. 2. April–June 1938. Published by the American Anthropological Society.

McGovern, Patrick. *Uncorking the Past: The Quest for Wine, Beer, and Other Alcoholic Beverages.* Berkeley: University of California Press, 2009.

Robinson, Sherry. *Apache Voices: Their Stories of Survival as Told to Eve Ball.* Albuquerque: University of New Mexico Press, 2000.

Baron, Stanley. *Brewed in America: A History of Beer and Ale in the United States.* Boston: Little, Brown and Company, 1962.

Erdoes, Richard. *Saloons of the Old West.* New York: Gramercy Books, 1979.

Oliver, Garrett, ed. *The Oxford Companion to Beer.* New York: Oxford University Press, 2012.

Mittelman, Amy. *Brewing Battles: A History of American Beer.* New York: Algora Publishing, 2008.

McGahan, A. M. "The Emergence of the National Brewing Oligopoly: Competition in the American Market, 1933–1958. *The Business History Review,* Vol. 65, No. 2. Published by the President and Fellows of Harvard College.

Pinsker, Joe. "Why Is American Beer So Bland?" *The Atlantic.* August 4, 2015.

CHAPTER 6: THE WEST COAST

Oliver, Garrett, ed. *The Oxford Companion to Beer*. New York: Oxford University Press, 2012.

Baron, Stanley. *Brewed in America: A History of Beer and Ale in the United States*. Boston: Little, Brown and Company, 1962.

Erdoes, Richard. *Saloons of the Old West*. New York: Gramercy Books, 1979.

Gilbert, Grove, Richard Humphrey, John Sewell, and Frank Soule. *The San Francisco Earthquake and Fire of April 18, 1906 and Their Effects on Structures and Structural Materials*. Published by the Department of the Interior, United States Geological Survey. Washington Government Printing Office, 1907.

Rueger, Theodore. "In Stricken Frisco: Description and Illustration of the Horror of Earthquake and Fire." *American Brewer's Review*. Chicago and New York, May 1, 1906, Vol. XX, No. 5.

McGahan, A. M. "The Emergence of the Brewing Oligopoly: Competition in the American Market, 1933–1958." *The Business History Review,* Vol. 65, No. 2. Summer 1991.

Carrol, Glenn, and Anand Swaminathan. "Why the Microbrewery Movement? Organizational Dynamics of Resource Partitioning in the U.S. Brewing Industry." *American Journal of Sociology,* Vol. 106, No. 3. November 2000.

Acitelli, Tom. *The Audacity of Hops: The History of America's Craft Beer Revolution*. Chicago: Chicago Review Press, 2013.

Ogle, Maureen. *Ambitious Brew: The Story of American Beer*. Orlando: Harcourt, 2006.

INDEX

Page references in *italics* indicate photographs and their captions.

Arizona Wilderness Brewing
Company, 190–91
Assize of Bread and Ale, 26
Aztecs, 193, 195–96, 235

Backer, Domine, 69–70
Balché, 192
Ballantine Ale, 165
Balsa River Valley, 193–94
Barbary Coast (San Francisco),
238–39
Barley
origins of beer, 4, *16*, 17, 98
use by Puritans, 36
use in Africa, 98, 98*n*, 100*n*
use in Europe, 60–61, 65, 136
use in Midwest, 153, 166, 169
use in the South, 89, 94, 98,
105, 106, 108, 113
use on West Coast, 243–44, 260
Battle of Little Bighorn, 171
Baumgardner Distillery, 99
Bavaria, 125, 128–39
Bavarian Brewery, 240
Bayard brothers, 66
Bayou Teche Miel Sauvage, 88
Bean, Roy, *206*
Beaver hats, *55*–56
Beekman, Gerard G., 77
Beer, use of term, 28–29, 28*n*
Beer bottling, 173–74, 220–21, 236
Beer canning, 207, 221–22, 226
Beer consumption, 3, 22–23, 157,
209, 220, 248, 265
Beer distribution, 175–76, 201–2
Beer gardens, 148–49, *150*, 156–57
Beer marketing, 170–71, *249*,
251, 252
Beer oligopoly, 250–52, 265*n*
Beer origins, 4, 15–17, 63, 103*n*, 131
Beer quality, 25–26, 30, 75, 79,
135–36, 138–39
Beer rations (rationing), 17, 23,
40–41, 57, 77, 105
Beer steins, 148, 148*n*
Beer–Wine Revenue Act of
1933, *220*

Belcher, Andrew, 48
Bell in Hand Tavern (Boston), 13
Benicia Brewery, 246
Beor, 19–20
Beowulf, 19
Berkeley Hundred Plantation, 95
Best, Jacob, 154
Best, Phillip, 179
Biddle, Clement, 77, 108
Biddle, John, 77
Black Death, 22
Blaxton, William, 45
Block, Adrian, 56
Blue Anchor Inn (Philadelphia), 73
Bock beer, 130, 130*n*, *155*, 207
Böhm, Johannes, 141*n*
Boone, Daniel, 112
Boorde, Andrew, 28
Bordley, J. B., 79
Boston, 11–13, 47–49
Harvard University, 8, 41–43
taverns, 39, 40, 40*n*, 46, 49
Boston Beer Company, 11–13,
11–15, *12*
Boston Bread riot, 47–48
Boston Harbor, 36
Boston Lager, 11, 12–13, *14*, 15, 261
Boston Massacre (1770), 49
Bowery (New York City), 156–57
Boyd, James, 79
Boyd, Robert, 79
Bradford, William, 32–33, 34–35
Brannan, Samuel, 237
Bratt, Dirk, 68
Brauer Gesellen Union, 172
Bremen, 129
Brewers Street (Manhattan), 65,
65*n*, 75
Brewer's yeast, 130–34, 139–40
Brewsters, *21*, 21–22, 23–24
Briggs, Richard, 41
Brigit, Saint, 110
British Celts, 109–11
British Isles, 15–29
Bronze Age, 17
Brouwershaven, 59
Brown, George, 208

Pequot Indians, 2
Perkins, Jacob, 175
Persimmons, 99–101, 99n
Philadelphia, 72–77, 141
　breweries, 73–74, 75–76,
　　79–80, 106–7, 144–45, 157
　Dutch settlers, 72–75
　German immigrants, 141, 144–45
Phoenix, 190, 205
Picts, 18
Pilgrims, 32–39, 63
Pilsners, 133, 139, 168–70, 169–70
Pisco Punch, 239
Pitson, James, 46
Pittsburgh, brewery, 80
Plantation of Ulster, 111–12
Plantation system, 97–104, 158–59
Plymouth Colony, 35–36
Pocahontas, 95
Pombe, 98, *100*
Porter, 27, 79–80, 107–8
Portland, 243, 260
Portsmouth Square (San Francisco), 238
Powhatan Indians, 63, 95
"Premium beer," 250
Printing press, 41, 42
Progressive Era, 210–11
Prohibition, 212–16, 218–19, 248
Protestant Reformation, 32–33, 137
Pulque, 193, 196, 199, 234
Pumpkin, 38–39
Puritans, 2, 8, 36–50, 102
Pyramid Breweries, 53–54
Pytheas, 17, 110

Rail transportation, 175–77, 201–2
Rainier Brewing Company, 226,
　249, 250
Raleigh, Walter, 94
Redhook Ale Brewery, 260
Red Lion Brewery, 66–67
Refrigeration, 174–77, 202, 206,
　208, 220–21, 244–45
Revere, Paul, 256
Revolutionary War, 76–78, 81
Reynolds, William, 43

Rheingold Brewing Company, 250
Rheinheitsgebot, 125, 136–37, 139
Rhode Island, 40, 69
Rice, 169
Roanoke Island, 94
Rodriguez, Juan, 69
Rogue Ales, 53–54
Rolfe, John, 95–96
Romans, ancient, 17–18, 56,
　126, 235
Roosevelt, Franklin D., *220*
Royal Society of London, 38
Rueger, Theodore, 246, 248
Rum, 46, 48–49, 74, 78, 101–2,
　104–5
Ruppert, Jacob, 54, 215, 222
Rutgers University, 66
Ruth, George Herman "Babe,"
　11, 54

Saccharomyces cerevisiae, 131–32
Saccharomyces pastorianus, 133–34
Sacramento, 242
Saguaro wine, 196
Saint-Crépin Monastery, 57
Ste. Genevieve, Missouri, 151
Saint Gall Abbey, 127
St. Louis, 153, 165–66
　breweries, 123, 154, 166, 182–85.
　　See also Anheuser-Busch
　German immigrants in, 147–50
Saint Trond Abbey, 57
Saloons, 208–9, 239–40
Salt Lake City, breweries, 205
Samuel Adams Boston Lager, 11,
　12–13, *14*, 15, 261
San Antonio, 202–4
San Diego Padres, 53
San Francisco, *245*, 253–58
　craft brewing in, 231–34, 254–58
　earthquake of 1906, 245–46,
　　247, 248
　Empire Brewery, 238–42
　Loma Prieta earthquake of
　　1989, 231
San Francisco Brewery, 240
Saxer, Henry, 243